sprinklers
& DRIP SYSTEMS

By Lisa Stockwell Kessler and the Editors of Sunset Books, Menlo Park, California

SUNSET BOOKS

VICE PRESIDENT, GENERAL MANAGER
Richard A. Smeby
VICE PRESIDENT, EDITORIAL DIRECTOR
Bob Doyle
PRODUCTION DIRECTOR
Lory Day
OPERATIONS DIRECTOR
Rosann Sutherland
MARKETING MANAGER
Linda Barker
ART DIRECTOR
Vasken Guiragossian
SPECIAL SALES
Brad Moses

STAFF FOR THIS BOOK
WRITER
Lisa Stockwell Kessler
MANAGING EDITOR
Esther Ferington
COPY EDITOR
Anne Farr
ILLUSTRATOR
Rik Olson
PHOTO STYLING
Laurie Scott, Jill Slater
PAGE PRODUCTION
Linda M. Bouchard, Janie Farn
PREPRESS COORDINATOR
Eligio Hernandez
INDEXER
Lina Burton
PROOFREADER
Joan Beth Erickson

COVER PHOTOGRAPHS
Top, Crandall & Crandall; bottom left,
Tom Wyatt; bottom middle, Dig Cor-
poration; bottom right, Saxon Holt
COVER DESIGN: Vasken Guiragossian

10 9 8 7 6 5 4 3 2 1
First Printing January 2006
Copyright © 2006 Sunset Publishing
Corporation, Menlo Park, CA 94025. First
edition. All rights reserved, including the right
of reproduction in whole or in part in any form.
Library of Congress Control Number
2005927070. ISBN-13: 978-0-376-03840-1
ISBN-10: 0-376-03840-3
Printed in the United States of America.

We gratefully acknowledge John Stokes and
Tom Bressan of The Urban Farmer Store in San
Francisco, who provided their expert knowledge
of irrigation and reviewed the manuscript.
For additional copies of *Sprinklers & Drip
Systems* or any other Sunset book, call 1-800-
526-5111 or visit us at www.sunset.com.

contents

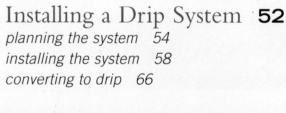

WATER SYSTEM CHOICES

There are many different ways to water a garden, from hand-watering with a hose to installing an automated irrigation system. In most cases, an irrigation system offers the best results. The system can be as simple as attaching a timer to one of your outdoor faucets and running a line of drip tubing from the timer to a flower or vegetable bed. Larger, more elaborate gardens may require an automated, multicircuit system.

Depending on your landscape needs, you can choose from an underground sprinkler system, an aboveground drip irrigation system, or a hybrid system that combines the two. The best solution for you and your garden will depend on several factors, including cost, ease of installation, and maintenance requirements. Most important of all, you should choose a system that can be tailored to the types of plants, number of planting zones, and specific conditions of your garden.

Whichever system you select, make sure that it is designed with the future in mind so that it can be expanded and adapted as plants grow or as you replace or develop planting areas.

saving water and time

Rainfall is vital to your garden's health—especially during the warmer months of the year, when plants need it most. Unfortunately, rain doesn't fall on schedule. Even in the wettest areas, you can't count on it to coincide with the needs of thirsty lawns, vegetables, and flowers conditioned to living in moist soil. And while some hearty, drought-tolerant plants can live a long time without water, all plants need regular water when they're getting established and some need water throughout the year—even more if they're grown in containers. So, almost any garden needs some form of supplemental watering.

Although you may be able to get by in a small garden with a hose or a portable sprinkler, such methods are time-consuming and hard to apply consistently. A well-designed irrigation system will free your time for other activities in the garden like planting, pruning, or relaxing. A system that is automated can also take care of your plants when you're not around to water them yourself.

Another important benefit of an efficient watering system is that it avoids habitual over- or underwatering—practices that can damage or kill plants. By controlling the amount of water you use, you not only limit your water bill but also avoid the cost and trouble of putting in new plants.

This map shows the average number of inches of rainfall recorded by weather stations in 24 cities between May 1 and October 31. The numbers clearly indicate how much drier the 12 cities west of the 100th meridian are than the 12 cities east of it during those critical 6 months. The darkest shadings on the map correspond to the greatest annual rainfall.

RAINFALL AMOUNTS BETWEEN MAY 1 AND OCTOBER 31

100TH MERIDIAN

TTLE 10.42
LAND 9.8
BILLINGS 8.78
BOISE 4.15
DULUTH 20.66
BOSTON 19.57
NEW YORK 21.32
CHICAGO 20.02
CLEVELAND 18.91
SALT LAKE CITY 6.11
OMAHA 21.72
RENO 2.29
SAN FRANCISCO 1.95
COLORADO SPRINGS 11.85
ST. LOUIS 18.47
NORFOLK 25.44
LOS ANGELES .86
PHOENIX 2.71
SAN DIEGO .94
ATLANTA 21.27
EL PASO 5.33
DALLAS 16.4
NEW ORLEANS 30.78
MIAMI 43.89

THE RIGHT AMOUNT AT THE RIGHT TIME

Delivering a consistent amount of water to your plants on a regular schedule promotes even growth and strong root systems. Most people know the danger of underwatering. Without water, plants can't absorb the minerals they need from soil or fertilizer. Plants that don't get enough water will wilt, lose their leaves, and eventually dry up and die. But overwatering can be just as harmful. Most plants need air around their root systems to breathe and will rot and die if their roots don't get enough oxygen. Too much water can also cause soil erosion or nutrient leaching, permanently degrading your soil. Plants that are over- or underwatered are also more likely to develop diseases or attract insects that can not only harm them but also spread to other plants around them.

WATER-WISE GARDENING

One way to minimize (though not eliminate) watering requirements is to select plants that grow naturally in your environment. For example, try to use drought-tolerant plants for semiarid and arid climates, thirstier plants for areas with significant summer rainfall, and water-loving plants for moist, semitropical regions. When you plant a garden filled with native species, you can look to nature to help you with your irrigation.

LEFT: Wilted, discolored foliage shows that these black-eyed Susans are suffering from lack of water. Over time, underwatering can cause permanent damage or even kill some plants. RIGHT: Too much water caused this thyme plant to rot, beginning at the roots and moving out. Overwatering is a risk when you leave a portable sprinkler or hose running and unattended.

WHERE YOUR WATER GOES

You may not think you're using much water when you spray the lawn or let a hose run into a collection of container plantings, but you're probably consuming it at a higher rate than you imagine. Here are some revealing statistics about typical garden water use:

■ A 20-by-40-foot area of lawn needs 2,000 to 4,200 gallons of water a month (some kinds of turf require more than others). In a climate with rainy summers, nature will provide much of that moisture; in an arid or semiarid region, artificial irrigation is required.

■ A ½-inch-diameter garden hose with no nozzle or attachment delivers as much as 300 gallons of water per hour; a ⅝-inch-diameter hose, as much as 500 gallons per hour; and a ¾-inch-diameter hose, as much as 600 gallons per hour.

■ An outdoor faucet with a slow-dripping leak can waste 350 gallons a month; one with a fast leak, about 600 gallons a month.

■ A standard full-circle lawn sprinkler head emits 2 to 4 gallons every minute it's in operation. Lower-precipitation models are available, but take longer to water the same area.

■ A typical drip emitter delivers water slowly, at a rate of about ½ to 2 gallons of water per hour, but covers a much smaller area than does a sprinkler head.

watering options

For years, underground sprinkler systems were the last word in home irrigation. In recent decades, an alternative has emerged—drip irrigation, which uses aboveground tubing. Each has its advantages.

The two types of systems are not mutually exclusive, and you can use both in one garden. You can also convert all or a portion of an existing sprinkler system to drip irrigation (see pages 66–67). Whatever system you use, plants with similar watering needs will ideally be grouped together so they can be served by separate irrigation circuits, allowing you to tailor the delivery of water to meet the plants' requirements.

If you live in an area with heavy summer rainfall, however, an installed system may be overkill. If you have just a few plantings to water during dry spells, you can automate a portable sprinkler or soaker hose by connecting it to a hose bibb with a control valve and manual timer.

SPRINKLER SYSTEMS An underground sprinkler system is best suited for watering large, thirsty areas such as lawns or big sections of uniform ground cover. You can also use sprinklers to irrigate flower or vegetable beds, as long as you have a multicircuit system to water each area separately. (You'll also need to avoid placing the heads so the spray is blocked by the plants as they grow.)

A sprinkler system is almost invisible, with most of the sprinkler heads flush with the ground when they're not in use. This makes it an attractive system—and also low-maintenance, since buried parts are less likely to sustain damage. Although sprinkler systems once had a reputation as water wasters, newer sprinkler heads apply water much more precisely.

Once installed, a sprinkler system can be a joy to have. But it must be planned carefully. Sprinkler systems need adequate water pressure and flow rates (see pages 30–31). And installing one requires digging trenches throughout your landscape.

THE DRIP ALTERNATIVE Water conservation is the most common reason people select a drip irrigation system. Since drip emitters and sprayers apply water much more slowly than conventional sprinklers do, a drip system largely eliminates water runoff and greatly reduces water loss through evaporation and overspray. The water also won't blow off course in windy conditions.

An underground sprinkler system provides even coverage to a smooth expanse of lawn. The pop-up spray heads drop out of sight when not in use.

Drip is also the best way to ensure consistent moisture to the roots of individual plants, making it well suited to watering flower and vegetable beds and to deep-root watering of shrubs and trees. And, although sprinklers are the usual choice for lawns, you can choose to install drip emitter lines underground instead (see page 65). Minisprayers installed in a drip system are effective in watering odd-shaped patches or narrow strips of lawn.

Drip emitters won't irrigate surrounding soil (encouraging weeds), and they won't spray leaves, petals, and trunks, where excess moisture can encourage fungal diseases. Drip is usually preferable on hills because the water is less likely to run off. Drip systems are also more accepting of low water pressure or flow rates.

Drip installation is easy in both mature and undeveloped landscapes, requiring no trenching or special tools. But drip irrigation is not an "out of sight, out of mind" system. Since all the tubing and components are exposed, drip systems may need adjustments or repairs after being kicked by running children, chewed by dogs, or hit by lawn mowers or other tools. The low-flow watering components also tend to clog more easily than sprinkler heads, requiring more frequent maintenance.

Drip irrigation waters diverse plantings across a varied terrain. The tubing at left will be hidden when the plants mature.

GOING HYBRID It's increasingly common to use both sprinkler and drip irrigation in one garden, sending sprinkler circuits out to a lawn or ground cover, for example, and drip lines to flower and vegetable beds, shrubs, and trees.

If you decide to use both sprinklers and drip irrigation, install them as described in chapters 3 and 4. Install enough control valves to operate all the sprinkler and drip circuits. Put in the sprinkler system first, since it requires trenching. Then run your drip circuits. The same timer can control both types of circuits.

sprinkler basics

The controller automatically opens and closes the valves for the different circuits according to a preset program.

There are two kinds of control valves: antisiphon and in-line. Antisiphon valves are installed aboveground, have built-in backflow preventers, and are used in warm climates where pipes won't freeze. Each must be installed at least 12 inches above the highest sprinkler in its circuit.

In-line control valves are installed underground and are protected in a valve box. They require a separate backflow preventer located at the start of the system. In-line valves are most often used in cold-winter climates where they can be protected below the frost line, but they are also used in hilly areas where valves can't be placed 12 inches higher than the highest sprinkler in a circuit.

Local codes may determine some aspects of the control valves you install, such as the material (plastic or brass) or whether the backflow preventer must be part of or separated from the valves.

Some codes require a special reduced-pressure (RP) principle backflow preventer. Check your local codes before making any purchase.

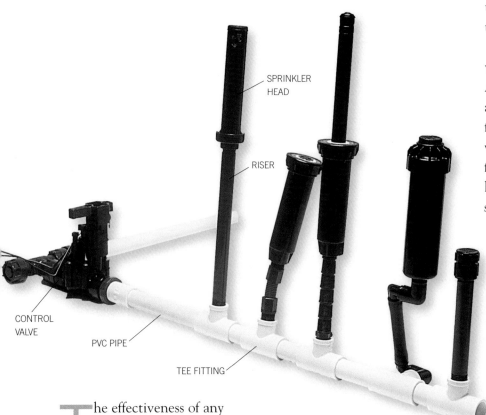

- SPRINKLER HEAD
- RISER
- CONTROL VALVE
- PVC PIPE
- TEE FITTING

The effectiveness of any sprinkler system depends on proper layout and installation as well as on the right components.

The system includes a main shutoff valve to turn it on or off, a controller or timer, and a backflow preventer, essential for preventing water from flowing backward into the water supply. Control valves control the flow of water to separate circuits made of pipes and fittings, risers, and sprinkler heads. (As described here, in some circumstances control valves also provide the backflow prevention.)

CONTROL VALVES

Control valves turn the water on and off to each individual circuit in the system. If you have more than one circuit, the valves are grouped together in a manifold. Operated by remote control, the valves are wired to a controller.

IN-LINE VALVE

ANTISIPHON VALVE

PIPES, FITTINGS, AND RISERS

The essential structure of a sprinkler system consists of pipes, fittings, and vertical risers. All are installed underground.

PIPE VARIETIES The main pipe material used for underground sprinkler systems is polyvinyl chloride (PVC). Schedule 40 PVC is used most often for sprinkler systems. For aboveground use near the start of the system, use Schedule 80 pipe, which is stronger and stands up better to sunlight than standard white PVC. Where it's impossible to run a rigid pipe, use flexible PVC, which can be cemented to Schedule 40 PVC. (Flexible PVC should not be used for lines under constant pressure.)

PVC pipe diameters of ¾ inch, 1 inch, and 1¼ inches are widely used for residential sprinkler systems. The diameter affects the flow rate and the pressure lost as water flows through the pipe; a supplier can help you select the right pipe for your job. You can also consult the chart on page 31.

In some areas, polyethylene (PE) may be used for the pipes that run underground to the sprinkler heads and PVC for the main supply line to the control valves (and, for aboveground valves, from the valves into the ground). PE is flexible and does not require the use of solvent cement, but it does not stand up

to pressure changes as well as PVC. Some local codes require that you use copper for the main supply line.

FITTINGS Fittings are used to make turns, branch a line in several directions, join pipes, and close off pipe ends. PVC fittings come in both threaded and slip types. Slip fittings are cemented with solvent, creating strong connections. Threaded fittings link pieces you may need to remove or replace, such as risers. When using threaded fittings, it is essential that your measurements be exact.

Fittings for PE pipe are barbed to insert into the pipe or threaded to join to other threaded parts. Connections are held in place with stainless steel clamps.

RISER OPTIONS Risers connect the underground line to the sprinkler heads. Options include flexible polyethylene risers precut to the desired heights, plastic cutoff types that give you a choice of heights, and threaded Schedule 80 PVC pipe.

Adjustable risers allow you to raise or lower a sprinkler head as needed over time. You can also raise sprinkler heads with cutoff riser extensions. Swing-joint risers allow you to adjust the height, angle, and placement of a sprinkler head easily during installation.

FLEXIBLE PVC

PVC WITH FLARED END

SCHEDULE 40 PVC

SCHEDULE 80 PVC

COUPLING

TEE FITTING

FLEXIBLE RISER

CUTOFF RISER

SWING-JOINT RISER

THREADED PVC RISERS

11

SPRINKLER HEADS

Sprinkler heads fall into three categories: spray heads, rotors, and bubblers. Always group the same type of heads in a single circuit to make sure the heads have the same approximate flow rate. As a rule, use heads with a small spray radius for small areas and heads with a large spray radius for large areas.

SPRAY HEADS Spray heads throw out a fixed spray with a radius of 5 to 15 feet, making them a good choice for precise, controlled watering of fairly small lawns, irregularly shaped beds, and shrubs. They have a higher precipitation rate than rotors, putting out more water over a shorter period of time. Spray heads are made up of two parts:

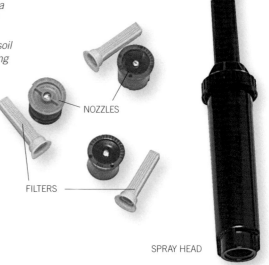

TOP LEFT: A spray head distributes water in a quarter circle. The spray pattern is determined by its nozzle. BOTTOM LEFT: A gear-driven rotor sends out a single stream of water as it rotates from side to side. ABOVE: A bubbler soaks the soil around a plant without wetting its leaves.

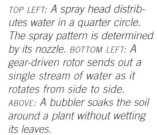

NOZZLES

FILTERS

SPRAY HEAD

the body and the nozzle. The body itself comes in two styles. The shrub type stays aboveground on a riser; the pop-up type stays hidden until the water goes on and then rises from 2 to 12 inches above the soil level. Nozzles come in a range of patterns, including full, half, and quarter circles. The nozzles screw onto the body above a removable filter and are usually sold separately.

Compared with rotors, spray heads operate at relatively low water pressures, from 20 to 30 psi (pounds per square inch). At higher pressures they tend to mist or fog. If you have higher water pressure, you may have to install a pressure reducer or use spray heads with flow-control adjustment.

ROTORS Rotors shoot out focused streams of water at long distances and at different trajectories. They require more water pressure to operate than spray heads (30 to 70 psi) and throw water substantially farther—from 15 to 50 feet. This makes them an economical choice for very large lawns and landscaped areas.

Today's rotors are gear-driven, making them much quieter and easier to maintain than the older impact-type rotors. Their closed cases reduce maintenance, since the cases keep out dirt and debris. Like spray heads, rotors have a variety of nozzles that make up different patterns and usually come free with each sprinkler head. They also come in both stationary shrub and pop-up body types.

Rotors deliver water more slowly than spray heads, an advantage for slow-draining clay soil. Although you'll have to run rotors up to 4 times longer than spray heads for a given area, you'll need fewer rotors in a circuit—and possibly fewer circuits. Rotors shouldn't be used in small areas, however, since they will overspray and waste water.

BUBBLERS Bubblers produce a downward spray of water up to 5 feet that soaks the soil beneath them. They are good for watering trees, shrubs, or planters when you want to reach the root zone but avoid wetting the foliage.

ROTARY NOZZLE ON
SPRINKLER BODY

POP-UP ROTOR

SHRUB ROTOR

BUBBLER ON RISER

tools for drip irrigation

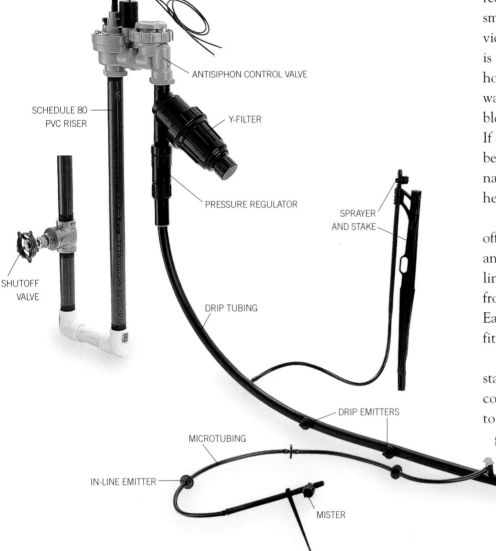

SCHEDULE 80
PVC RISER

ANTISIPHON CONTROL VALVE

Y-FILTER

PRESSURE REGULATOR

SHUTOFF
VALVE

SPRAYER
AND STAKE

DRIP TUBING

DRIP EMITTERS

MICROTUBING

IN-LINE EMITTER

MISTER

END CAP

requires a filter to prevent the small openings on the water devices from clogging. Also needed is a pressure regulator to adjust household water pressure downward; otherwise, fittings may blow apart under excess force. If desired, a fertilizer injector can be attached as well. The combination of these parts is called a head assembly.

You can run a single drip line off a head assembly attached to an outdoor water faucet, or send lines to different planting areas from separate control valves. Each drip circuit includes tubing, fittings, and watering devices.

Many irrigation companies sell starter kits that come with all the components and tools you need to install a drip system in your garden. It is an economical way to get started, and once you have the main drip line down, you can buy additional tubing and emitters as needed.

TUBING AND FITTINGS
Within each circuit, tubing and fittings carry water from the head assembly to different parts of the landscape.

TUBING Solid-walled drip tubing, also called drip hose, is the standard way to distribute water from the control valve onward. (Be-

I n a typical drip irrigation system, water flows through lengths of flexible polyethylene tubing. Emitters or sprayers attached to the tubing deliver water to the root zone of each plant in a gradual flow adjusted for the plant's water requirements. The flexible tubing used in a drip system resists damage from the sun's ultraviolet (UV) rays, and fittings are simply pushed into place.

The water output rate of drip watering devices is so slow that it is measured in gallons per hour (gph) rather than the gallons per minute (gpm) of traditional sprinklers. Most devices work best at 15 to 30 psi, although some require even lower pressure.

Like sprinkler systems, drip systems can be operated by controllers operating one or more control valves (see page 10). Additionally, each drip circuit

cause drip tubing isn't strong enough for lines that are under constant pressure, use PVC for any pipes running from your water source to the control valves.) Drip tubing is laid directly on the ground, its dark color generally inconspicuous. While the tubing can be hidden by mulch, it should not be buried underground—moles and gophers will chew right through it.

Drip tubing is made of flexible black polyethylene and is available in ½-inch and ⅜-inch diameters. Polyethylene tubing is flexible enough to snake through plantings and loop around trees and shrubs. It is also resistant to the sun's ultraviolet rays and has a life span of 15 to 25 years.

The ½-inch size is generally used for the main drip line from a control valve and carries up to 320 gph. The ⅜-inch size is more flexible and easier to hide and is often used for lines that branch off the main line or lines to water container plants. It carries up to 100 gph. When buying tubing, check the inside and outside dimensions. Fittings for one brand of tubing may not fit another brand.

You may insert emitters directly into the tubing or install them in smaller, ¼-inch microtubing—sometimes called spaghetti tubing—that branches off the drip tubing. (Avoid ⅛-inch microtubing, which tends to clog.) Microtubing is available in either polyethylene or high-grade vinyl

and has a flow rate of around 15 gph. A punch is used to make holes in drip tubing to install couplings or emitters.

Emitter line, an increasingly popular alternative, consists of tubing in which emitters have been preinstalled.

FITTINGS Drip fittings are color-coded by size: red for ⅜-inch tubing, blue and green for two different sizes that are sold as ½-inch tubing. (Neither is actually ½ inch, and the two are not interchangeable.) Make sure to use the right size of fitting for your tubing so the fittings won't blow out when the water is running.

Use couplings to join two sections of tubing when you wish to expand a drip circuit or splice damaged tubing. Elbows are useful for making neat sharp turns around features such as deck corners or raised walkways. Adapters make the transition between drip tubing and PVC pipe.

Connecting polyethylene tubing and drip fittings is easy; you simply push them together. Three styles of fittings—compression, barbed, and locking—are available for ½- and ⅜-inch drip hose; barbed fittings are used for ¼-inch microtubing. Both compression and barbed fittings are designed to stay put once the insertion is made. People with limited strength in their hands will appreciate the locking type, for which no force is needed.

⅜" BARBED FITTINGS

⅜" SHUTOFF VALVE

½" COMPRESSION FITTINGS

¼" MICROTUBING SHUTOFF VALVES

¼" BARBED FITTINGS FOR MICROTUBING

WATERING DEVICES

Watering devices called emitters let water drip or ooze onto the root zone; others spray water into the air like miniature sprinklers. Emitter line does double duty, both carrying and emitting water.

DRIP EMITTERS Emitters drip water directly onto the soil at the plant's root zone. Most emitters have barbed ends that snap into $\frac{1}{2}$-inch or $\frac{3}{8}$-inch polyethylene tubing, or can be pushed into the ends of microtubing. In-line emitters can be inserted between lengths of $\frac{1}{4}$-inch tubing alone or in a chain.

DRIP EMITTERS

There are many different emitters on the market that vary in output rate as well as in shape, size, and internal mechanism. Most types dispense $\frac{1}{2}$, 1, or 2 gallons per hour (gph). Emitters are color-coded by water output; the tubing delivering the water always goes into the colored side of the emitter. Unlike sprinkler heads, emitters with different output rates can be used in a single circuit to accommodate different plants' watering requirements. By choosing emitters with slower drip rates, you can place more in a single zone or run a longer line of tubing.

For a large or sloped garden, consider investing in pressure-compensating emitters. These emitters deliver a precise amount of water regardless of changes in pressure along a line, and they rarely clog because a flexible diaphragm inside regulates the water flow and flushes particles from the system. If you have a dirty water supply or very hard water, use either pressure-compensating emitters or non-plugging turbulent-flow emitters, a lower-priced alternative.

Some emitters can be adjusted to increase their flow from delivering droplets to a gentle stream of water, a feature that is especially useful for plants growing in sandy soil or porous container mixes. There are also emitters that sit almost flush with $\frac{1}{2}$-inch tubing, limiting the chance of damage. Others come with a built-in stake to hold them just above the soil. You can also buy multioutlet emitters to run microtubing to nearby plants.

EMITTER LINE Emitter line is tubing with emitters preinstalled at regular intervals inside the tube. It comes in two sizes: $\frac{1}{2}$-inch drip tubing and $\frac{1}{4}$-inch microtubing. Sturdy and long-lasting, emitter

line is less expensive than tubing and emitters purchased separately, and it provides a slow, even output of water. The $\frac{1}{2}$-inch size is a practical choice for watering hedges, vegetable beds, and densely planted flower beds; the $\frac{1}{4}$-inch size is better for window boxes and large containers.

SPRAYERS, MINISPRINKLERS, AND MISTERS Drip system sprayers water more slowly and operate at a much lower pressure than conventional sprinkler heads. Drip sprayers consist of small spray heads that fit into the ends of ¼-inch tubing, rigid risers, or pop-up risers. They're useful for irrigating closely spaced or dense plantings, such as ground covers and flower beds. They also dispense water efficiently over the root zones of trees and shrubs and deliver the right amount of moisture to hanging plants.

Like sprinkler heads, sprayers are available in quarter-, half-, and full-circle patterns, as well as a bow-tie shape. Some sprayer heads come with threaded barbs, ready to connect to risers, spikes, or tubing; others are already attached to a stake or pop-up assembly. Different sprayers have output rates from 5 to 30 gph and may cover a 4- to 25-foot radius.

Minisprinklers cover larger areas than sprayers, spraying water in partial or full-circle patterns measuring from 10 to 30 feet across. (Rotary versions of minisprinklers are available, but should not be used in the same zone with sprayers.) Some minisprinklers are nonclogging and self-cleaning. Because the spray consists of larger droplets than that of sprayers, it is less affected by the wind. Output ranges from about 6 to 50 gph.

Misters raise the humidity around

fog-loving plants such as fuchsias, azaleas, and bonsais, and can be used to slowly water hanging plants. They can be either staked in the ground to spray upward or suspended above a hanging plant to spray downward. Their water output rates range from 2 to 10 gph.

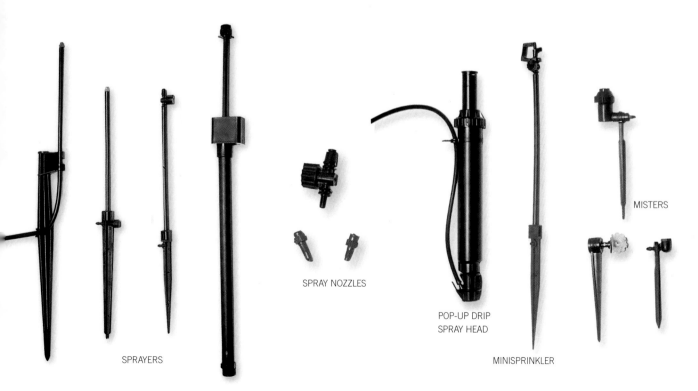

SPRAYERS

SPRAY NOZZLES

POP-UP DRIP
SPRAY HEAD

MINISPRINKLER

MISTERS

automating the system

Any irrigation system you install can be turned on manually or automated with a timer. The beauty of automation is that you can keep your plants healthy without having to remember when and for how long to water them. You can schedule your system to water at any time of the day or night and even program it to water when you're away on vacation.

The heart of an automated watering system—the controller or timer—is a mechanical or electronic clock that automatically regulates the operation of each sprinkler or drip circuit connected to it. The simplest controllers turn on and shut off the flow of water at a single faucet. These are useful for a single-circuit system or to control one small area, like a deck or patio with container plants. More versatile controllers let you set the watering frequency and duration of every circuit in your landscape.

MECHANICAL TIMERS Simple mechanical timers automate water shutoff, but because they have no power source or memory, you must set them every time you want to water. Most types attach directly to a hose bibb or to a hose-Y. Simply turn the dial to the desired watering time. The timer usually has an override setting to enable you to use the faucet normally.

BATTERY-OPERATED TIMERS A battery-operated timer attached to your hose bibb or hose-Y will turn your system on and off at designated times. Depending on the model, you may be able to schedule the timer to turn on at intervals (such as every third or fifth day) or on certain days of the week. Some models will repeat short cycles up to several times a day. Most battery timers can control just one circuit

hooked to the hose bibb, but you can also buy timers that connect to your faucet and control up to four circuits, each with its own start time and duration.

You can purchase battery-operated timers with dials that let you set a program, or with digital readouts and keypads for punching in your program. Look for a model that has a "low battery" indicator; the timer's memory will fail when the batteries do.

MECHANICAL TIMER

BATTERY-OPERATED
TIMER

MULTIPROGRAM ELECTRONIC TIMER

3-STATION EXPANSION MODULE

WALL-MOUNTED ELECTRONIC TIMERS

Wall-mounted electronic timers permit the most flexibility in scheduling both the duration and the frequency of watering. They plug into a 110V power receptacle. Some models are designed for outdoor installation; others must be installed indoors. Low-voltage insulated cable connects the irrigation system's control valves to the timer.

Electronic timers range from a multicircuit controller, in which a limited number of circuits run sequentially, to one with multiprogram capability. A program defines the watering frequency for each circuit. A single program allows you to use each circuit the same number of times a day or week. Multiprogram models allow you to use each circuit independently; so, for example, one circuit can be set to water a lawn three days a week for two short intervals, and another to water a hedge once a week for a longer duration. Unless all your planting areas have the same irrigation needs, you should purchase a timer with the capacity for separately programming multiple circuits or groups of circuits. If you have sufficient water pressure and flow, you can also get a timer that can operate two valves with separate programs at one time.

The more features a controller has, the more expensive it will be. Some useful features to consider include battery backup, so the clock and program information is retained if the power fails, and expandability, so you can add circuits as your landscape grows or changes. A very valuable addition is a rain sensor (below), a small device that attaches to the outside of your house and shuts off the irrigation system if it detects too much rain. It monitors the amount of rainfall and cuts off the controller when the rain reaches a predetermined level. Rain sensors work with most electronic timers.

Some controllers come with remote controls so that you can program the timer from a distance—an advantage when the controller is located in a dark corner of your garage. The most sophisticated models have a seasonal adjustment feature that lets you alter the programmed run times from 10 to 150 percent of their current settings.

FIRST STEPS

Before you shop for irrigation supplies or dig trenches through your landscape, you need to collect some important information. What different plant zones do you have in your garden? How much moisture do your plants need? What kind of soil do you have? What weather conditions exist in each part of your garden? How much water do you have to work with? This chapter will help you assemble the answers you need to develop an effective irrigation system.

With the information you collect, you will be able to draw up a detailed garden plan from which you or an irrigation contractor can develop an irrigation layout tailored to the specific needs and conditions of your landscape.

assessing watering needs

The key to a healthy and productive garden is to plant species that will thrive in your general climate as well as in your property's micro-climates—all of the climates within climates created by changes in elevation, prevailing winds, and sun and shade patterns. Ideally, plants that need little or no irrigation will be in one area of the garden and plants that require regular moisture in another. In this way, you avoid underwatering some plants and overwatering the others. By organizing your yard into "hydrozones"—groups of plants with similar watering needs—you'll simplify irrigation while giving your plants the amount of moisture they need for good health.

In a well-designed garden, high-water-use plants are located nearest the house and patio, with plants requiring less water progressively farther away. The great advantage of this layout is that you don't have to extend an irrigation system to the outer reaches of a large yard. Also, if some of the most drought-tolerant plants look a little scruffy, it won't matter, because they'll be viewed mainly from afar. If the plant groupings in your garden do not fall into obvious hydrozones, you may want to do some transplanting before you install an irrigation system.

The following pages suggest watering guidelines and strategies for some of the most common plant groupings. Keep in mind that all plants need more water in the first year or two after they are put in the ground and that some plants may continue to have special watering needs.

This landscape includes a variety of hydrozones, each with its own irrigation needs. The container plants and lawn both require short, frequent watering; different flower beds should be watered longer but less often.

These irregularly shaped sections of lawn could be watered with low radius pop-up sprinklers, positioned to provide full coverage without overspraying the walkway.

LAWNS

Some kinds of turf are more drought-tolerant than others, but most lawns demand lots of water during warm weather. Unless you live in a climate with regular summer rain, you'll need to irrigate.

Turf grasses need moisture at the root zone, which is fairly shallow—usually 4 to 6 inches deep. If you apply so much water that it seeps farther down into the soil, the water is wasted. Turf grass is healthiest when its roots are allowed to dry out between waterings. The usual way to irrigate lawns is with sprinklers—either portable or an underground system—although you can run underground drip emitter line as an alternative (see page 65). Whether you use a sprinkler system or drip irrigation, the lawn should be treated as a separate hydrozone and watered with its own circuit or circuits.

To water a lawn with a sprinkler system, try "pulsing" your irrigation by dividing the total watering period into several shorter intervals to allow time for the water to soak into the soil. This is especially useful if you find that water runs off before it can soak in. If that is the case, also check to see if your lawn has thatch buildup that is repelling water or if the soil has become compacted.

GROUND COVER

A ground cover is any low-growing, dense plant that blankets the ground and binds the soil. Ground covers are often used as alternatives to lawns because their roots sink deeper and don't require as frequent watering.

How a plant grows determines whether you treat it individually or as a mass planting, like a lawn. Some ground covers send out horizontal branches. They should be treated as individual plants, even though they may give the impression of a uniform planting when closely spaced. The best way to water them is with a drip emitter line, because water placement is more precise and the line can be hidden from view.

Ground covers that spread by underground runners or branches that root are difficult to identify as separate plants. It's better to water these plants as a mass, with portable sprinklers, a sprinkler system, or sprayers in a drip system. (In a small area, parallel emitter lines will also work.) Be sure to account for the mature height of the ground cover. Pop-ups only rise about a foot, so if the plants will grow higher, use shrub-type sprinkler heads on adjustable risers. For ground covers on slopes, choose low-precipitation heads or drip sprayers. Use drip-system sprayers for narrow or tight plantings.

A large expanse of dense ground cover is best irrigated by a sprinkler system with low-precipitation rotors.

Drip sprayers water a hillside flower bed slowly without creating runoff.

FLOWER BEDS

Flowering plants are often grouped together in beds, but they don't necessarily have the same watering needs. Annuals need constant watering until flowering is finished. Perennials need regular moisture from the onset of growth until they finish blooming, and then some moisture from the end of bloom until dormancy. After that, some perennials tolerate routine watering. Others do better under—or may actually require—drier conditions.

Because of the differing watering needs of flowering plants, the best way to irrigate them is generally with a drip system with individual emitters. Drip irrigation also keeps the flowers and leaves dry. If you install a separate drip line within a hydrozone for your drought-tolerant plants, you can remove it after the first year or so, when those plants no longer need watering.

Some flowers are more prone to disease when kept consistently moist, and tall flowering plants will fall over from the weight of sprayed water. If you irrigate with drip sprayers or an underground sprinkler system, use flat-head sprayers that send the spray out straight rather than up. Run them early in the morning so that leaves will dry by midday.

TREES AND SHRUBS

When watering trees and shrubs, you need to get water to their root systems, which are generally within the top 2 feet of soil. The roots of established plants extend out beyond the plant canopies, so mature trees and shrubs benefit from water applied at or just beyond the drip line (the line where rainfall drips off the edge of the canopy to the ground); watering too close to the trunk invites rot. However, the root system will be closer to the trunk when a tree or shrub is first planted. You need to adjust the position of watering devices as the plant grows.

The easiest way to irrigate trees and shrubs is with a drip system.

Stake a ring of ½-inch emitter line at the tree's drip line, and enlarge the ring as the plant grows. For a line of trees or an orchard, run two parallel lines of tubing about 3 feet on either side of the trunks and insert emitters into the tubing below the canopy. This will encourage balanced root growth. For a newly planted tree, use two drip emitters above the root ball, then shift to emitter line after the plant is established. In sandy soil, use one or two drip sprayers attached to the drip tubing to cover the entire root zone of a tree.

A circle of emitter line waters a tree's roots without wetting the trunk.

VEGETABLE BEDS

Most vegetables do best with their roots kept moist and their leaves dry. You'll be able to water more efficiently if you plant your vegetables according to their water needs. Group them by how big they get and how fast they grow; the bigger and faster-growing they are, the more water they'll use. Of the shallow-rooted vegetables, the leafy ones need a little more water than root crops.

Don't mix new plantings of a crop with existing ones, as seedlings and mature plants have different irrigation needs. Young ones must be watered as often as two or three times a day for a short period, whereas larger ones need more water, to a greater depth.

In climates where there is ample summer rainfall, you can use soaker hoses to supplement the rain. In all other climates, the best way to keep vegetable roots consistently moist is with a drip system. A drip emitter line with emitters 12 inches apart works when vegetables are planted in rows or close together. In a wide bed, run parallel emitter lines 16 inches apart. When drip lines are spaced farther apart, use solid tubing and place a single emitter at the base of each plant.

Parallel runs of emitter line are enough to keep a vegetable bed moist.

Certain vegetables, such as salad greens, do best with overhead water. If they are placed together, run drip tubing along the edges of the bed and attach sprayers so that the spray from one overlaps with the next one.

CONTAINER PLANTS

Potted plants have less soil from which to draw moisture and their roots are restricted by the pot size, so they require more frequent irrigation than do the same plants in the ground. Hanging pots require even more frequent watering, because the air circulating around them dries the soil faster.

When irrigating container plants, moisten all the soil, not just the top few inches. You'll know the soil is saturated when water runs freely from the drainage hole. If it drains too fast, though, it's probably running through air spaces between dried-out soil and the container walls; submerge the container in a tub of water for about half an hour.

An automated drip system makes it easy to water a collection of pots. Treat containers as a separate watering zone, since they should be watered frequently for only 2 to 5 minutes. Run microtubing from the main drip line into each pot. Depending on the container, you can connect the microtubing to one or more drip emitters, to a ¼-inch emitter line that encircles the plants, or to a small adjustable bubbler, mister, or sprayer. Since loose potting soil lets water run straight down, use several emitters spaced about 6 inches apart in all but the smallest pots.

Using an elbow fitting flattens and protects microtubing at the rim of a planter.

microclimates, soil, and slope

It is rare that a garden is completely uniform in weather conditions, soil type, and terrain. A good watering system will take into account all the varying conditions of your specific landscape as well as the type of plants it needs to irrigate.

WEATHER CONDITIONS

Because trees, fences, and other obstructions can cast shadows or block wind—slopes can keep out wind, too—different areas in your garden experience different conditions throughout the day. Wind, sun, and shade all affect the amount of water your plants need to thrive, so it's important to consider the microclimates of your garden before installing any watering devices.

WIND Strong winds can quickly rob plants of moisture and blow sprinkled water off course. If you have any area that is chronically windy throughout the year or season, treat it as a separate watering zone and apply water close to the ground with emitter line or drip emitters. You can also protect your plants with a windbreak—a barrier that slows or dissipates the wind.

A solid barrier (right, top) makes a poor windbreak. Because wind "flows" like water, it comes over the top of a solid barrier in a wave, crashing down on the other side. The best type of windbreak

is one that lets some wind pass through, such as a lattice fence or a tall informal hedge (below). As the wind filters through the fence openings or the shrub branches, it loses force.

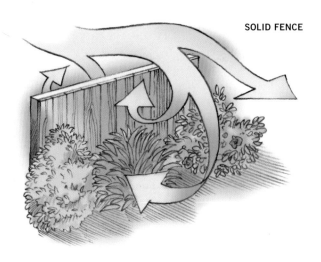

SOLID FENCE

LATTICE FENCE

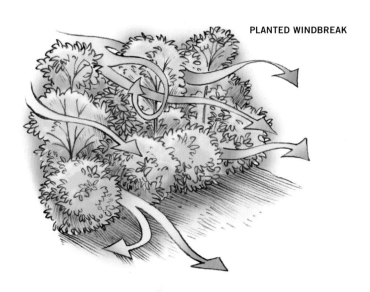

PLANTED WINDBREAK

SUN AND SHADE It's important to evaluate how many hours during the day a garden area is in full sun, partial sun, or shade. Beyond the fact that some plants need sun or shade to grow, direct sun causes moisture in the air and soil to evaporate faster. Shade keeps soil cool and helps retain its moisture. Therefore, a sunny site, especially one that gets strong afternoon sun, will need to be watered more frequently and for longer periods than a shady one and should be considered its own watering zone. You can minimize evaporation in a sunny area by applying a layer of insulating, organic mulch over the soil. In hot weather, mulch also helps to moderate soil temperature, encouraging steady root growth.

ABOVE: A garden in full sun may require daily watering, especially during the hot summer months. *BOTTOM:* A shady site helps maintain the moist, cool soil that shade plants require; irrigate it more lightly and less often.

ASSESSING SOIL TYPES

Not all soil absorbs water the same way. While all soil contains the same ingredients—mineral particles, living and dead organic matter, and pore spaces for water and air—it contains them in different proportions. When you know the characteristics of your soil, you can select the best water delivery methods for it.

If you're uncertain what type of soil you have, you can have a sample analyzed at a soils laboratory. This is also recommended if you suspect you have problem soil. Usually, however, it's enough to do a simple test by wetting some soil and squeezing it into a ball. If it crumbles, your soil is sandy. If it sticks firmly together, it's clay. If some of the ball holds its shape but breaks apart easily, you have loam.

SANDY SOIL "Light," sandy soil has large pores, so water enters easily and moves through it quickly, leaving the soil well aerated. However, sandy soil does not hold water well, which means that you must water it frequently during dry weather. Overwatering sandy soil results not in runoff or plant damage but rather in waste—water and nutrients will quickly wash down below the plants' root zone, where they do no good. The best way to water when you have sandy soil is with sprinkler heads or drip sprayers for short intervals or with drip emitters spaced closely together, about 12 inches apart.

CLAY SOIL A soil that's high in clay contains particles that pack closely together, leaving little pore space for either water or air. Often referred to as "heavy" soil, clay absorbs water slowly and causes it to puddle quickly and run off. Once wet, however, clay soil retains water well. Plants growing in clay can go longer between waterings than those in other soil types. If you don't keep that in mind, you can easily overwater them. Low-flow drip emitters— $1/2$ or 1 gph—spaced 18 to 24 inches apart are a good choice for clay soil. If you are using a sprinkler system, select low-precipitation sprinkler heads that apply the water slowly.

LOAM Loam has a good balance of minerals, organic matter, and pore spaces, with all the advantages of sandy and clay soils but none of the drawbacks. This almost perfect soil is easy to wet, dries out at a moderate rate, and is well aerated. Water will spread slowly and evenly through loam, making most watering methods efficient.

HOW MUCH SLOPE?

SOIL ABSORPTION PATTERNS

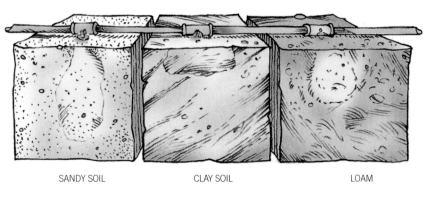

SANDY SOIL   CLAY SOIL   LOAM

This comparison of three soil types shows how each would absorb water dripped from an emitter. Water has less sideways movement in sandy soil, requiring irrigation sources to be spaced closer together.

13½'

2'

MEASURING SLOPE

Excessive slopes in a landscape (over 10 percent) can be a problem for gardeners. One way to deal with them is to create flat terraces held in place by retaining walls. If you decide to plant on a slope without making structural changes, be sure to irrigate with low-precipitation devices set at the appropriate angles.

To determine whether a slope exceeds 10 percent, stake one end of a long piece of string to the high point of your terrain. Extend the string out horizontally to the point just above the low point of the slope and, using a level, adjust the string until it is completely level. Now let the other end of the string drop down to the ground, held taut by a weight attached to it. The horizontal and vertical lines of string should form a 90° angle. Have a helper measure the length of the horizontal string and the height of the vertical length of string.

Dividing the vertical distance of 2' by the horizontal distance of 13½' yields .15. Multiply by 100, and the result is the percentage of slope—in this case, 15 percent.

The percentage of slope is calculated by dividing the vertical rise or height by the horizontal run and multiplying by 100.

For a very large sloped area, judge by eye whether the slope is about the same throughout; then measure the slope within a smaller, more manageable section using the same methods.

REMEDIES FOR PROBLEM SOILS

If your soil doesn't drain well or has too much salt, try the following remedies:

HARDPAN is an impervious layer of soil. The closer it is to the surface, the more trouble it causes: it prevents water from draining and keeps plant roots shallow. Try breaking through the layer with an iron bar or a soil auger. If that doesn't work, landscape professionals can sometimes help by creating subsurface drainage or drainage chimneys with special equipment. If that's too much work or too expensive, you can plant in raised beds or mounds filled with good soil.

COMPACTED SOIL has few pores in it for water or air to enter. Rototill the area to a depth of 18 inches.

SALTY SOIL is common near the seashore and in arid climates, or where fertilizers and manure have been overused. You can eliminate many salts by periodically leaching the soil. If the excess salt is sodium, however, it bonds to the soil particles and can't just be washed way. To solve this problem, incorporate gypsum (calcium sulfate) into the soil. The calcium will displace the sodium. The soil should then be irrigated well to wash away the dislodged sodium. If you aren't sure what kind of salt you're dealing with and don't want to send a sample to a lab, always add gypsum before leaching. If your water supply is salty, leaching won't work, and you may have to settle for salt-tolerant plants.

pressure and flow

The final pieces of information you need to collect before planning your irrigation system relate to the water supply. You'll need to find out both the water pressure and the flow rate. Water pressure is the force that pushes the water through the pipes. If the pressure is too low, it may not operate certain sprinkler systems. If it's too high, it can cause drip systems to malfunction or drip lines to burst. Therefore, knowing what you have is critical to creating a system that will work properly. The flow rate is a different measurement; it's the amount of water available in a given time period and will dictate how many plants can be watered at once.

DETERMINING WATER PRESSURE

Water pressure is measured in pounds per square inch (psi). Normal household pressure is around 40 to 50 psi, but it can vary widely. Some homes have readings as high as 100 psi. Most sprinklers won't work efficiently if the pressure is too low; most are designed to work best at 30 to 50 psi. Many

PRESSURE GAUGE

drip systems require a pressure range from 20 to 40 psi. You can adjust the pressure to suit either type of system (below, left), but the first step is to find out if that's necessary.

To measure your home's water pressure, screw a water-pressure gauge onto an outdoor faucet. Then turn off all other water outlets throughout your house, including dish- and clothes washers. (Don't flush the toilets as you measure the pressure, either.) Turn the outdoor faucet on full and record the psi reading. Repeat the process at each outside faucet location, taking several readings throughout the day. To be conservative, use the lowest reading when calculating sprinkler output.

ADJUSTING PRESSURE LEVELS

If your water pressure is too high for the type of irrigation system you want, or if it's causing sprinkler heads in an existing system to mist or fog, you can easily fix the problem. Either a pressure regulator for your entire system or individual pressure-reducing valves will restrain the force to a sustainable level—and also reduce wear on your equipment. (For very high water pressure, however, you may wish to consult a plumber or your water supplier; high pressure can be harmful to interior plumbing fixtures as well.)

Low pressure is a problem for some sprinkler systems. Installing a booster pump in your main irrigation supply line will increase the pressure enough to accommodate rotors and other high-pressure sprinkler heads. For efficiency's sake, you can wire a switch called a pump-start relay to the sprinkler circuits needing high pressure; it will activate the pump only when valves operating those circuits are turned on. Drip circuits will normally work at low water pressures without additional equipment.

EFFECTS OF ELEVATION ON WATER PRESSURE

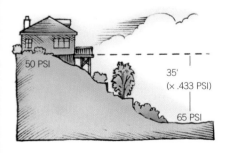

Water is delivered to both houses shown at 50 psi. But water traveling through irrigation pipes to their backyard gardens will lose pressure in the case of the upslope garden and gain pressure in the case of the downslope garden.

30

Keep in mind that water gains or loses force as it travels down- or uphill (opposite, below). Water also loses pressure through friction as it rubs against the interior walls of pipes, valves, fittings, and other irrigation components. The solution to minimizing pressure loss through friction is to avoid using overlong pipe runs or too high a flow rate. If necessary, break a large irrigation circuit into smaller ones to ensure the pressure you need to run your system.

DETERMINING FLOW RATE

Flow rate, the amount of water that moves through pipes in a given period of time, is measured in gallons per hour (gph) or gallons per minute (gpm). All types of sprinkler heads and emitters have designated output rates

(expressed in gph or gpm), so planning a system is, in part, a matter of assigning only as many devices to a given circuit as your water supply can handle. If you have planned for a sprinkler circuit that requires a higher flow rate than you have, the solution is to create several separate circuits. Flow rate isn't as critical a factor for drip irrigation as it is for a sprinkler system, because comparatively little water is dispensed.

The easiest way to determine flow rate is with a bucket. First, fill a bucket with a gallon of water and mark this level on the bucket's inside wall. Empty the bucket, then place it under an outdoor faucet, turn the water on full force, and count how many seconds it takes to fill to the line.

Then, divide the total number of seconds into 60 to determine the gallons per minute (gpm). This figure is your flow rate. Although the test will work with a 1-gallon bucket, it is far more accurate with a 5-gallon bucket. Just remember to divide the final result by 5.

Test the flow rate at every faucet around your house you might use for irrigation. Flow rates may differ between faucets as a result of their location as well as the diameter, type, and length of the pipe behind the faucets. If you use more than one faucet for your irrigation system, select the one with the highest flow rate for the larger number of circuits.

FINDING PIPE SIZE

Using the appropriate size of irrigation pipe for your flow rate will help keep friction, and thus pressure loss, to a minimum. Don't use a smaller-diameter pipe size than indicated, though you can choose a larger one—in fact, sizing up can help compensate for low pressure or very long pipe runs. Find the pipe material you plan to use and the flow rate you've measured; at the bottom of that column you'll see the appropriate pipe size.

PIPE MATERIAL	MAXIMUM FLOW RATE (GPM)					
Schedule 40 PVC	4	8	13	22	30	50
Schedule 80 PVC	3	6	11	20	26	46
Polyethylene drip tubing	4 (240 gph)	8 (480 gph)	13 (780 gph)			
Recommended pipe size	½ in.	¾ in.	1 in.	1¼ in.	1½ in.	2 in.

drawing up the plan

Once you have grouped your plants into watering zones, evaluated your microclimates and soil conditions, and collected your plumbing data, you are ready to draw up a garden plan. Your garden plan shows the existing situation you have to work with; it's an important step toward creating your irrigation layout—your plan for an irrigation system to be added to the garden.

ELEMENTS OF A GARDEN PLAN

A garden plan is a scale drawing that shows your property in relation to your house. It includes all planting areas, trees, shrubs, and raised beds; streams and ponds; and fences, walkways, patios, decks, and any other structures that might block the path of pipes or the spray of sprinkler heads.

It also includes any significant slopes and the location of outdoor faucets—or the location of the home's main underground supply line, if you plan to connect there.

MEASURING Depending on the size of your property, use a 50- or 100-foot tape measure and measure the relevant areas to the nearest foot. Deviations of just a few feet can cause real problems when it comes to having accurate lengths of pipe or tubing. Measurements must be especially accurate for sprinkler systems.

Start by measuring your home's exterior dimensions. Then measure straight lines from each corner of your house to the property lines. Note these dimensions on a rough sketch. The lengths and widths of any concrete, stone,

or brick walkways or sitting areas should be noted. If you have a septic tank and leach field, also indicate their locations and dimensions.

Next, measure the areas to be watered, including flower beds, lawns, raised beds, and patios or decks with containers. Now mark the location where you intend to tap into your home's water supply. Finally, indicate where you want to locate the controller or timer, if not on the faucet itself.

Once you have the measurements, redraw the sketch to scale on graph paper, making each square equal 1, 2, 4, or 5 feet, depending on your garden's size.

ADDING HYDROZONES On a copy of your garden plan (it's a good idea to make a master and several copies, in case you make a mistake when adding details), break the planting into hydrozones by circling each zone in a different color.

Once you have entered these details on your garden plan, indicate any slopes. You may also note which areas are in sun or shade and which experience windy conditions. You are now ready to begin laying out your irrigation system. You can do this yourself using the information on pages 36–43 and 54–57 or you can take the plan to an irrigation specialist or retailer. Some stores will create a layout for free if you purchase their products.

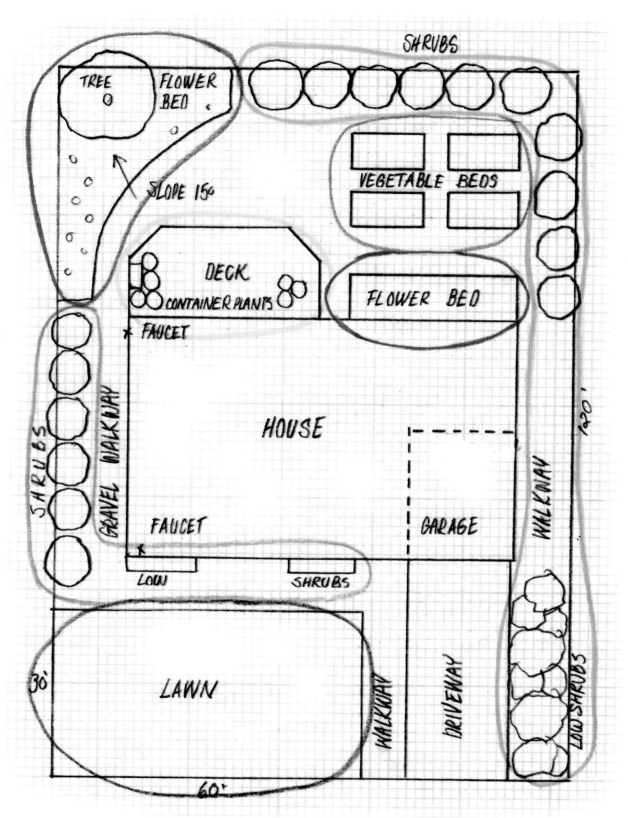

Within the drawing (as labels):

SHRUBS

TREE

FLOWER BED

SLOPE 15°

VEGETABLE BEDS

DECK

CONTAINER PLANTS

FLOWER BED

FAUCET

SHRUBS

GRAVEL WALKWAY

HOUSE

WALKWAY

FAUCET

GARAGE

LOW

SHRUBS

LAWN

30'

60'

WALKWAY

DRIVEWAY

LOW SHRUBS

120'

A scale drawing of your property should include your house and your property boundaries, the plant-ings to be irrigated, significant slopes, the location of all water sources, and any possible obstructions such as walkways or decks. (This plan matches the landscape on the opposite page.)

INSTALLING A SPRINKLER SYSTEM

nstalling a sprinkler system takes care, but it's not an impossible task for most homeowners. In fact, it's a lot like putting together a set of plastic construction toys. The materials have become so easy to handle that the real work is not in the assembly but in the planning and the digging. Good planning is essential to deliver water properly to your plants and lawn.

Once you've drawn up a garden plan (see chapter 2), your next step is to select the right sprinkler heads for your landscape and place them appropriately. Following the steps in this chapter, you can then develop an irrigation layout for your new system and, finally, install it. Or, you may prefer to get professional help with the planning, plumbing connections, or digging.

The beauty of a well-planned sprinkler system is that once it is installed, it should operate with minimal maintenance for years to come. Try to plan so that you can expand the system as necessary. If you can't afford to cover your entire landscape, for example, start by installing a basic system in your lawn or selected flower beds. Then add to the system over time.

planning a new system

Before making any decisions about your system, call your local building department. Find out whether there are codes that affect its design, including the type of backflow preventer, valves, or pipe you can use and any restrictions on installing the system. Also call your utility companies to mark the locations of any underground gas, water, or telephone lines that run through your property. Record the location of all buried lines on your garden plan.

The first step in planning your sprinkler system is to determine the water source, which is almost always your home water supply (see page 43 if you're considering a pond instead). You'll also need to select the point at which to connect your irrigation system, as described on pages 42–43.

Make sure to check your water pressure and flow rate (see pages 30–31). If you have water pressure below 40 psi, you will be limited in the type of sprinkler heads you can use. Pressures between 80 and 100 psi may require some pressure or flow regulation to avoid misting at the sprinkler nozzle.

CHOOSING SPRINKLER HEADS AND RISERS

Now that you've developed a garden plan, the next step is to decide which sprinkler heads to use in each hydrozone.

In general, you'll be choosing between fixed spray heads and rotors. If you have a 30-foot-wide lawn, you're better off using rotors that throw that distance, rather than twice as many spray heads that distribute water only half as far. Conversely, if you have a

A large rectangular lawn is watered by single-stream quarter-arc rotors in each corner.

ABOVE LEFT: *A swing-joint riser is ideal to use wherever there is heavy foot traffic because it absorbs impact.*
ABOVE RIGHT: *A high riser ensures that tall plants nearby won't block water from covering the entire flower bed.*

10-foot-wide area, using a rotor with a 15-foot minimum radius would water areas beyond the lawn. If you have a large lawn but lack adequate water pressure for rotors, you may want to compare the cost of installing a booster pump with that of increasing the number of sprinkler heads and circuits.

But there are many variations on both rotors and sprinkler heads. Consider the following:

■ For open lawn areas where you intend to walk, play, or mow, install pop-up heads that automatically rise when the water goes on and drop down flush with the soil when watering is finished.

■ For a windy area, use a low-angle or flat-spray head, and keep the head as close to the ground as possible. Rotors are not practical in windy conditions.

■ For slopes, place low-precipitation rotors at the top of the hill. Because water delivered at the top runs downhill, less irrigation is needed near the bottom of the slope. A very long slope may require two or more lines of sprinkler heads, each controlled by its own valve, so that the lower lines can operate for less time than the upper ones.

■ For the lowest point in every circuit, install a sprinkler head with a preinstalled check valve. This will minimize drainage at the end of the irrigation cycle.

■ For heavy clay soil, select sprinkler heads with lower precipitation rates to prevent puddling and runoff.

■ For water with high levels of hard minerals, choose irrigation heads designed not to clog—and maintain them conscientiously.

■ For systems with high water pressure, use spray heads with pressure-compensating devices, preventing fogging and drift.

RISER CHOICES Sprinkler heads should be high enough that their spray is not blocked by growing plants. Where risers are likely to be bumped, use a flexible nipple at the base of the riser. Pop-up heads are best mounted on swing-joint risers, which allow you to adjust the top of the sprinkler head so that it is flush with the soil. Swing-joint risers are also less likely to break if the sprinkler head is abused.

PLOTTING SPRINKLER HEADS

When you've determined the suitability of different kinds of sprinkler heads for your garden, it's time to go back to your garden plan. Make several copies before you start. You'll be working out the number and location of sprinkler heads as well as the pipe layout.

Tackle one hydrozone at a time. (For a combination system, plot only the sprinkler circuits now. Drip circuits can be added later, as described in chapter 4.) Sprinkler heads come in a range of throw distances and patterns, so you have a lot of flexibility in designing a system that works well for your landscape. Start with square or rectangular spaces; free-form areas and curves take a little more consideration. Your goal is to use as few sprinkler heads as possible to achieve good coverage of each zone. The more heads you use, the more circuits you may have to create, which adds to the cost of the system.

A simple twist changes the spray pattern of a variable-arc spray nozzle.

A strip-pattern spray nozzle waters a narrow, rectangular space when placed at the side or in the center of the lawn or bed.

HEAD-TO-HEAD COVERAGE The most important rule in placing sprinkler heads is to always overlap their sprays. The spray from one head should extend all the way to the adjoining one, an arrangement called head-to-head coverage. To make this work, you'll need to space the sprinkler heads evenly within a zone.

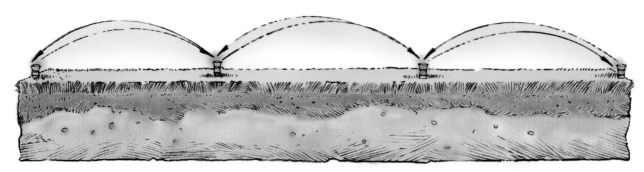

For uniform coverage, the spray from one sprinkler head should reach the adjoining head.

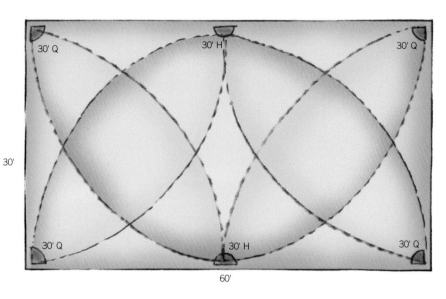

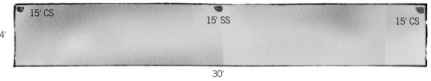

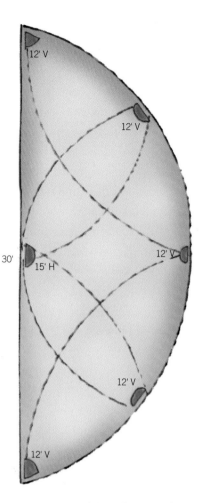

Rotors with quarter (Q) and half (H) arcs are the most efficient way of watering a large rectangular lawn (top). A narrow strip gets full coverage with one side-strip (SS) and two corner-strip (CS) spray heads (above). A circular area can be covered with a series of variable (V) spray heads, adjusted to fit the curve (right).

RECTANGULAR SPACES In regular, four-sided areas, mark sprinkler locations first in the corners and then, if needed, along the perimeter.

The proportions of some areas make placement easy. For example, a 30-by-60-foot lawn can be covered by six 30-foot rotors—one in each corner and one in the middle of each 60-foot side (see above).

For dimensions that don't divide so neatly, start with a sprinkler head in each corner and then figure the fewest heads that each long side requires, based on the maximum throws for spray heads or rotors. If the area is wider than the throw distance of your chosen sprinkler

heads, place heads down the middle of the section as well.

NARROW STRIPS AND SPACES A long and narrow lawn or garden strip can be irrigated with a strip-pattern spray nozzle that throws out a rectangular, rather than a circular, spray. Three specialized shapes can be used to provide head-to-head coverage. A side-strip nozzle is positioned along the long side of the strip, a center-strip (opposite, top right) is located in the middle, and a corner strip, which has a spray arc that is essentially half of a side strip, is placed in the corner. Only corner strips and a single side strip are needed in the example above. Most strip-pattern

sprays cover widths of 4 to 5 feet and lengths of up to 30 feet.

IRREGULAR AREAS For irregular or curving areas, use spray heads that come with adjustable-pattern nozzles. You can usually play with the spray patterns to fit the area. In some cases a series of equally spaced sprinkler heads won't provide full coverage, and you'll have to add one head with smaller or greater coverage to fill the space. If you can't avoid some overspray, make sure it is kept to a minimum and does not hit your house, tree trunks, fences, or other surfaces that could be damaged by too much moisture.

PLOTTING THE CIRCUITS

The next step is to plan for pipes to supply the sprinkler heads. Ideally, each hydrozone in your landscape will have its own irrigation circuit, but some may require more than one. Make sure that in any given circuit all sprinkler heads are the same type and are rated for the same output. Do not mix spray heads and rotors, for example, or rotors with high precipitation and low precipitation.

As a rule of thumb, the total output for the heads on one circuit should not exceed 75 percent of the available water flow at the faucet to ensure there is adequate pressure to drive the sprinklers. For example, if your measured flow rate is 12 gpm, no single circuit should exceed 9 gpm.

To calculate the total output for a proposed circuit, you will need to know the output of each sprinkler head. You can get this information from the sprinkler manufacturer's workbook. Write the output of each sprinkler head in gpm next to its location on your plan. Working with one hydrozone at a time, assign as many sprinkler heads to a circuit as you can without exceeding the allotted flow. For example, if you have an available flow rate of 9 gpm, you could have up to 18 sprinkler heads with an output of .5 gpm each or up to five with an output of 1.8 gpm each.

If a circuit exceeds the flow limit, split the circuit into two. Alternatively, allocate some of the sprinkler heads to a circuit that still has some available flow, as long as they are the same type.

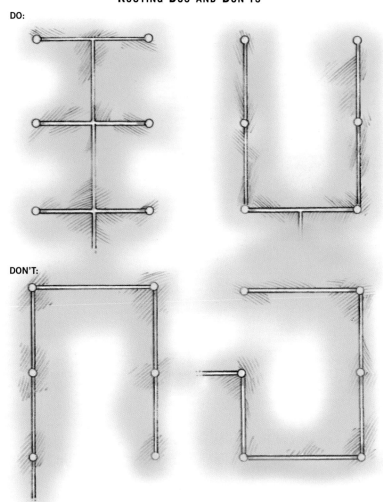

DO:

DON'T:

In the four drawings, pipe is being routed to six sprinkler heads. The H- and U-shaped routes are efficient. In the poorly laid out routes, the water must run through six sprinkler heads, which would significantly diminish its pressure by the time it reached the last sprinkler head.

ROUTING THE PIPE

Once you've grouped your sprinklers into circuits, sketch in the pipe runs on your layout. The first run of pipe is from the water supply connection to your control valves. How you lay out the pipe for each circuit will affect the performance of your system (above). To minimize pressure loss, avoid unnecessarily long runs. On a slope, lay as much pipe as possible horizontally rather than up and down.

If at all possible, avoid routing pipe through areas with many tree roots or under driveways or other pavement. Running a pipe under a driveway may require removing and replacing part of the driveway and installing a conduit.

WORKING FROM YOUR IRRIGATION LAYOUT

Your irrigation layout should now show the locations of sprinkler heads, control valves, and pipe. If you have measured your garden accurately and the plan is drawn to scale, this layout should give you all the information you need to assemble a shopping list.

List how many control valves and how many of each type of sprinkler head you have specified. The number of valves determines the size of the manifold system. Carefully measure the total length of pipe you need, then add 1 foot for every 20 feet of pipe to account for any minor miscalculations in your measurements.

List one threaded riser for each sprinkler head. Review your irrigation layout to note all required fittings, including a threaded tee or elbow for every riser, and elbows and crosses for bends and branches in the circuit. If you are using in-line, rather than antisiphon, valves, remember to buy a backflow preventer for the entire system. Always buy a shutoff valve. You'll also need pipe-thread tape for the threaded connections and PVC primer and cement to make slip connections.

Working on a copy of your original garden plan, first plot the location of your sprinkler heads and their spray areas (top right). Then use another copy to note the location of the control valve or valves for your sprinkler system and sketch in the pipe runs, producing your sprinkler irrigation layout (bottom right).

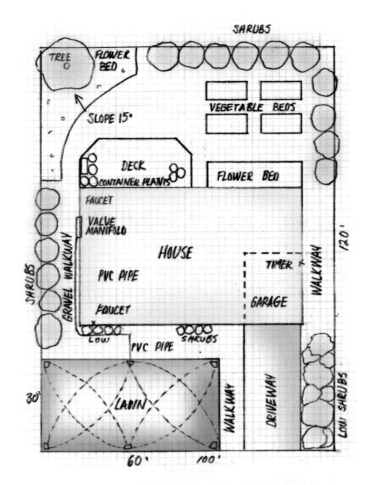

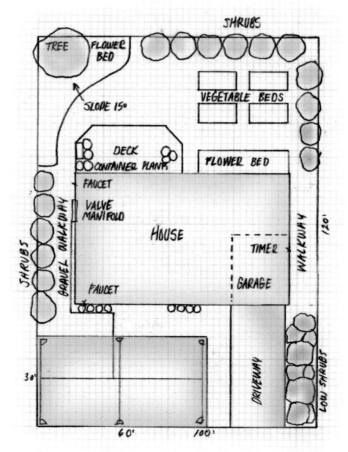

connecting to water

To supply a new sprinkler system, you'll have to tap into your existing cold-water supply system. If your plan calls for cutting existing pipes, you may prefer to hire a plumber to do the job. If you do decide to tackle it yourself, be sure to turn off the water supply before you begin any work.

WHERE TO START THE SYSTEM

In mild climates, you may tap into an outdoor faucet. In cold-winter climates, or if you don't have adequate water flow at the faucet, you can cut into your main supply line.

CUTTING IN AT AN EXISTING FAUCET

Often the easiest course of action is to make the connection at the pipe serving the faucet. With this method, you avoid cutting pipe. Turn off the house water supply and drain the faucet, then remove the faucet and install a brass or galvanized tee. Match the outlet sizes to the faucet pipe and the irrigation pipe you plan to use. Reattach the faucet; then install a nipple (a short length of pipe threaded at each end) in the stem of the tee fitting and connect a shutoff valve to that.

CUTTING IN AT THE SERVICE LINE

To attach to your main supply line before it enters the house, first shut off the water before the point where you will be cutting. For an aboveground connection, as illustrated here, remove a short section of pipe in the supply line, leaving just enough of a gap to slide on a slip tee. Install a nipple in the stem of the tee and attach a shutoff valve to it.

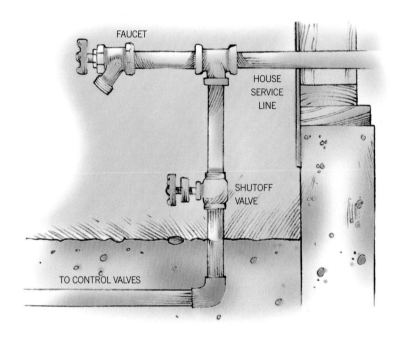

FAUCET

HOUSE SERVICE LINE

SHUTOFF VALVE

TO CONTROL VALVES

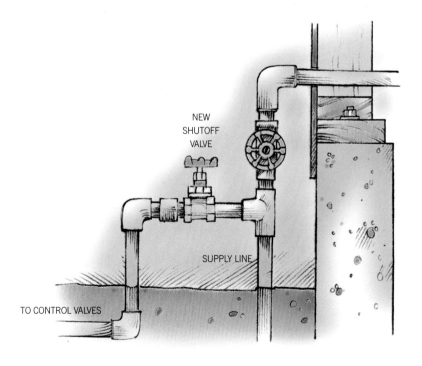

NEW SHUTOFF VALVE

SUPPLY LINE

TO CONTROL VALVES

BACKFLOW PREVENTION

Whenever you attach to a potable water system (like your indoor plumbing), always install a backflow preventer to prevent used water from flowing back into the water supply. If you are using antisiphon control valves, a preventer is built into each valve. For a single-circuit system that runs directly off the hose bibb, you can screw a vacuum breaker onto the end of the faucet. In-line valves need a pressure vacuum breaker at the start of the system, as long as it is located higher than the highest sprinkler head. Otherwise, you'll need to install a reduced-pressure (RP) principle backflow preventer on the main line before the valves at a point at least 12 inches above the ground.

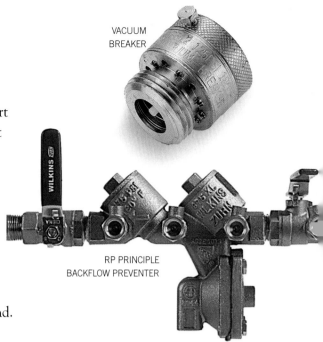

VACUUM BREAKER

RP PRINCIPLE BACKFLOW PREVENTER

ALTERNATE WATER SOURCES

Homes supplied with well water can be connected to irrigation systems just like those with city water; the only difference is how measurements of flow rate and pressure are taken. Local ponds can sometimes provide a water source, too.

WELL WATER If you don't have records of your well's flow rate, measure it at an outdoor faucet (see page 31). Be sure to run the water long enough for the pump to come on and stay on before starting. If the flow is less than 10 gpm, you may be limited to installing a drip system. Measure the water pressure with a pressure gauge on the wellhead pipe. If it's too low, you may need to replace your well pump with a more powerful one or install a booster pump.

SURFACE WATER If you have water rights to a pond, river, or stream on your property, you may be able to use it for irrigation. However, unless the water is elevated above your garden, you'll need a pump to move it. Before you consider using a private source of water, be sure it's appropriate for plants and poses no health threat to humans. Use a suitable heavy-duty filter to remove algae, sand, and other materials that would clog irrigation components.

the installation

The best time to install a sprinkler system is before you do any landscaping. In an established garden, avoid disturbing tree roots and move any plants in the areas where you plan to route your pipes. Weekend gardeners can install a system one section at a time; don't worry if you can't get it all in at once.

STAKING THE LANDSCAPE

Working from your irrigation layout, stake the location of all your sprinkler heads with flags or colored stakes. When they are all in place, use chalk, paint, or staked string to mark the lines where you will run your pipe, referring to your scale drawing for the proper layout. Make sure to include the location of the line that runs from the water supply pipe to the control valves and of any trench required to run wire from the valves to the timer.

After you've marked your lines, go back and remeasure all of them to make sure the actual and planned distances are the same. Make sure that sprinkler heads in each circuit are positioned to provide head-to-head coverage. The distance between flags should be equal to the throw of the heads.

DIGGING THE TRENCHES

The first major installation step is to dig trenches along the lines you have marked. The first one will go from the point of connection to the control valves.

In mild climates, trenches 8 to 12 inches deep are adequate. A trench depth of 18 inches is sufficient in most areas where hard freezes occur. In very cold climates, consult a local irrigation supplier to find out how deep you need to dig to be under the frost line. Trenches should be as straight and flat as possible.

Digging is heavy, disruptive work. Before you start, study your layout to make sure you haven't missed an opportunity to use a single shared trench for pipes that lead to separate circuits. A sturdy, flat shovel and pick are all you need to dig trenches by hand, but a rented trenching machine will make the job easier. Soften up hard ground by watering it with a portable sprinkler a few days before you begin.

To salvage sod, gently work the spade beneath the sod and peel it away before digging deeper. Put the sod you want to reuse on plastic bags or a tarp on one side and the excavated

Mark the location of your sprinkler heads with flags or colored stakes. The distance between them should be equal to the radius of the heads you will be using.

ABOVE: *A trenching machine digs through undeveloped areas or existing lawns quickly and efficiently.*

TOP LEFT: *The simplest way to dig a trench is with a sturdy, flat-headed shovel.* LEFT: *Set soil on a tarp to make easy work of refilling your trenches.*

soil also on plastic or a tarp on the other side. This will make it easier to replace the sod and soil after you've laid the pipe.

If you have a large area to cover, you can rent a trenching machine, which makes quick work of digging channels to the appropriate depth. A trenching machine is ideal for lawns and undeveloped areas, but don't use one to dig in ground covers or flower beds or you'll destroy your plants. You can also hire someone to use a pipe puller that pulls already connected runs of PVC pipe through the ground. (This is not a job for a novice.)

DIGGING UNDER A PATHWAY The best way to excavate under a pathway is to create a tunnel with a strong blast of water. An inexpensive kit that contains a power nozzle and fittings will allow you to drive a length of PVC pipe through the soil (left). A more expensive boring machine with a water-powered drill bit will also do the trick. As an alternative, you can attach a length of threaded galvanized steel pipe to a garden hose, aim it under the walkway, and turn on the water full force. Remove the pipe once the soil is wet enough, cover the end of a PVC pipe with duct tape to keep the soil out, and feed it through the hole. Afterwards, remove the tape.

MANIFOLD SYSTEM

INSTALLING CONTROL VALVES

To automate your sprinkler system, you will need a control valve (see page 10) for each circuit. For a multicircuit system, the best place to locate the control valves is in a manifold near the house. This facilitates wiring the valves to the timer. Choose a spot out of the line of spray in case you have to reach a valve while the system is operating. You may locate one manifold in the front yard and another in the back, but that will require two timers, or a long run of wire from one of the manifolds. If your water supply has a flow rate of more than 8 gpm, use a 1-inch pipe from the point of connection with the water supply to the control valves and circuits. If the flow rate is lower, you can use ¾-inch pipe.

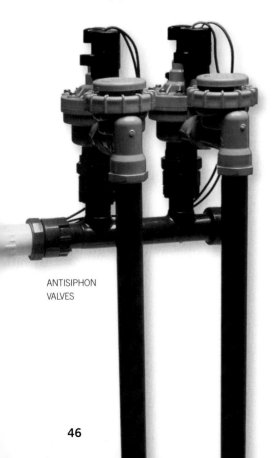

ANTISIPHON
VALVES

MANIFOLD SYSTEMS Inexpensive ready-made manifold systems enable you to put valves close together and remove them for servicing without cutting any pipe. Made of Schedule 80 PVC, modern manifold systems generally come in two-, three-, and four-valve outlets, but can be added to as needed.

ANTISIPHON VALVES The simplest way to attach a manifold system containing antisiphon valves is to install a tee (the pros say "tee off") at your hose bibb at least 12 inches above the highest sprinkler head. Attach a shutoff valve and then attach the manifold system just after the valve or on a threaded Schedule 80 PVC pipe extension. Once it's in place, attach your control valves to the manifold. The valves use threaded unions with gaskets, so no tools, glue, or pipe-thread tape is required.

Once the valves are in place, run threaded Schedule 80 PVC risers from the valves down to the trench, where you will connect them with the sprinkler pipes.

IN-LINE VALVES If you're using in-line valves, first install a vacuum breaker or reduced-pressure back-

flow preventer at the start of the system (see page 43). From there, run your main line straight down and then along the trench to the point where you want to locate the valves. Dig a hole a little bigger than the valve box, and line the hole with gravel to act as a drain. Make the top of the box even with the soil so you can have access to the valves.

Attach the in-line valves to the manifold, but don't connect it to the main line yet. First, place it in the valve box and mark the position of the valve outlets. Cut holes in the valve box for the pipe to run through. Return the manifold to the box and connect it to the main line.

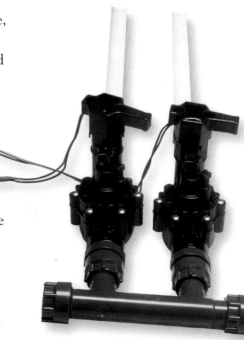

IN-LINE VALVES

WIRING THE VALVES Low-voltage insulated cable (typically AWG-14 or 18) that is approved for direct burial is used to connect the control valves to the timer. Use color-coded multistrand wire; a different-color wire joins each valve to the timer, and another color (usually white) links all the valves to the timer. Thus, if you have four valves, you'll need five-strand wire. If you may be expanding your system, get wire with extra strands so you won't have to rewire the whole system later.

Connect the wire as shown in the illustration at bottom right, running the wire underground to the timer location. If a trench is running in the same direction, lay the wire there, placing it beneath the pipe for added protection. Leave plenty of slack as you lay the wire, looping the wire around each valve and at turns in the trench. At the timer site, bring the wire aboveground and use cable staples to secure it along walls, joists, and other surfaces as needed. Leave the timer unplugged and turned off until the system is completely installed.

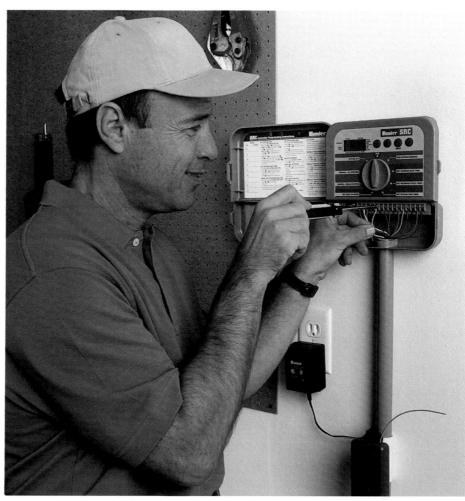

Connecting the valves to the timer will be much easier if you use color-coded irrigation wire.

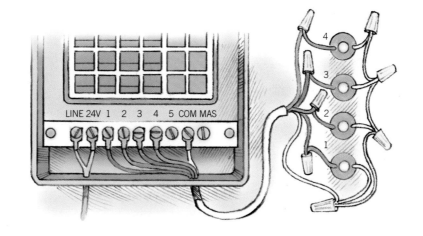

From the top of each control valve, connect one of the two wires to the common wire that connects all control valves. Connect the second wire to the desired station number screw on the timer, and attach the common wire to the common-wire screw terminal. Be sure to make a note of which station number goes to which circuit.

LAYING PIPE

From this point on, installation involves measuring, cutting, and gluing—tedious but not difficult work. The pipe should be laid as flat as possible at the bottom of the trench, though a little unevenness won't be a problem. As you work, try to keep the inside of the pipes as dirt-free as possible. When carrying lengths of PVC pipe, don't knock them together or drop them. The pipe can break—or worse, develop a hairline crack that you won't notice until it bursts under normal water pressure when the system is running.

From the control valves, run the pipes for each circuit. For long, straight runs, you can use pipes with straight and flared ends, rather than connecting the lengths with couplers. If you live in a cold-winter climate, install drain valves along the pipe at the lowest points in the run. Install the valves pointing downward and line the area below and around them with gravel. The valves will open when the line pressure drops below about 3 psi.

Measure and cut the pipes to run between fittings at the riser locations, bends, and other locations as needed. Allow enough length for pipe ends to fit inside the fittings.

You can lay out all the pipe lengths and fittings first and then go back to make the connections, or you can connect as you go along. Either way, check the location of each fitting against the irrigation layout as you work. Install PVC pipe according to the steps shown here.

1 Cut pipe
Use PVC ratcheting cutters for clean cuts. A hacksaw can leave plastic shards inside the pipe that can clog the system. Take care to make sure the cut is straight.

2 Position pipes
Prop the ends of pipe on spare lengths of PVC set across the trench (in this example, a cut end is being attached to the flared end of another pipe; to attach two cut ends, use a coupling). Propping up the pipes not only makes them easier to work with but keeps dirt out of them. Be sure both pipe ends are clean.

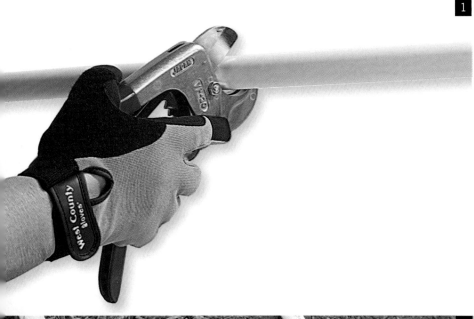

3 Apply primer

Before gluing PVC, spread a layer of PVC primer (often called purple primer) around the end of the pipe and also inside the flared end down to the shoulder. The primer should dry in a minute or so.

4 Apply solvent cement

Once the primer is dry, it's time for PVC solvent cement. Work quickly, as the cement sets within seconds. With a soft applicator brush (one is normally supplied with the container), apply the cement liberally to the pipe, then more lightly to the flared end.

5 Secure the connection

Quickly slip the pieces together, then immediately twist them partway around, to make the connection secure. Hold the pipes for a few seconds while the cement sets. Wipe off excess cement with a damp rag. Wait at least 6 hours before running water through the pipes—and even longer under cold, damp conditions.

INSTALLING RISERS

With a tape measure, determine the desired height of each sprinkler head. The top of a pop-up sprinkler should be level with the soil surface, and the riser for a stationary sprinkler should be high enough that foliage won't block the spray. If you use a cutoff threaded riser, cut it to the desired height and recheck the height after it is cut. Wrap the riser threads with pipe-thread tape and screw it into the tee fitting.

FLUSHING THE SYSTEM

Open the shutoff valve that supplies the irrigation system. Next, briefly open the control valves by hand to purge any dirt, PVC shards, or dried glue, which often clog new sprinkler systems. With the trenches still open, work quickly. Avoid letting the water run for as long as you would to flush an established system, and don't flood the trenches.

ATTACHING THE SPRINKLER HEADS

Screw rotors and spray-head bodies to the risers, making sure not to get any dirt into the pipes. Most spray-head bodies come with flushing caps that have a hole big enough to allow any debris still in the system to escape. Flush the system again and then replace the flushing caps with the appropriate nozzles.

FINISHING THE INSTALLATION

Congratulations! You've installed your own sprinkler system and are almost ready to enjoy your hard work. But before you sit back and relax, there are a few last steps.

TESTING THE SYSTEM

Before you fill in the trenches, test the system. First, turn off any water running in the house so that you don't have a water-hogging dishwasher or washing machine competing with your irrigation system. Make sure the shutoff valve to the irrigation system is open. Now turn on each circuit manually at the timer. Check that each circuit works, and that each sprinkler head is spraying freely, without obstruction. If a circuit does not come on, check the wiring connections and make sure the control valve wasn't installed backwards.

If a sprinkler head isn't working, remove it and check for clogging (see page 78). If that doesn't fix the problem, review your plans to verify that the head is really on the circuit you're testing. When several heads near each other barely spray, you may have made a mistake in assigning too many sprinkler heads to that circuit. Check whether they exceed the allowable flow; if so, you'll need to rethink the layout or remove some of the heads.

Next, make sure the sprinklers are providing even coverage. Remember, each head should throw water all the way to the adjacent heads. You may have to adjust a sprinkler's direction, throw, or spray pattern. Spray direction can often be easily altered by turning the sprinkler body or tweaking the riser. Most spray nozzles have an adjusting screw to control the distance the spray is thrown. You can adjust the spray pattern easily with variable nozzles, but not with set-pattern ones. To adjust a rotor's arc, follow the manufacturer's directions.

BACKFILLING THE TRENCHES

Once the system is working properly, carefully backfill the trenches. Fill each trench to just below the original soil or sod line, then flood it with water to settle the soil. Add more soil, mounding it slightly, then tamp with a hand tamper until it is even with the soil or sod around it. In a lawn, replace any sod you removed.

Sections of sod are easy to replace in a trenched lawn when they've been removed in even blocks and kept moist.

INSTALLING A DRIP SYSTEM

One of the great advantages of a drip system is that it takes no special skill to install. No trenching is necessary, and the tubing and fittings connect without the need for precise measurements and solvent cement. The one thing you will have to do before laying out the system is determine the size of each circuit and the type of tubing and emitters you will need to use to deliver water efficiently to each plant.

Whether a drip system will serve your entire landscape or operate in tandem with a sprinkler system, this chapter gives you everything you need to help you install drip circuits easily. It also provides information on converting part or all of a sprinkler system to drip.

If you have already installed an underground sprinkler system and are simply adding some planned drip circuits, you can probably do the job in a day. A stand-alone drip irrigation system will take a little longer, but can be installed in a weekend if you plan ahead.

planning the system

Whether you are installing a single line of drip tubing or a multicircuit system, a little planning is needed before you roll out the system. Start with your garden plan (see page 33), making some spare copies before you mark it up. If all the plants have roughly the same watering requirements and your garden is small, a single circuit can handle your entire drip system. Otherwise, you'll need at least one circuit per hydrozone.

SELECTING DRIP COMPONENTS

Different drip watering devices are better suited to different hydrozones. For more recommendations on choosing the right ones, see pages 22–25 and 28–29.

Individual drip emitters are useful for watering widely spaced plants, whereas emitter line and sprayers are better for closely

Four common drip solutions are illustrated below. TOP LEFT: A length of ¼-inch tubing with an emitter runs from ½-inch tubing to each container plant. TOP RIGHT: Spirals of ¼-inch tubing encircle shrubs. BOTTOM LEFT: Parallel lines of ½-inch emitter line run along straight rows of vegetables. BOTTOM RIGHT: Drip sprayers keep a large area moist.

spaced plants. Use emitter line for watering rows of plants, shrubs, or trees. Opt for drip emitters or emitter line to keep foliage dry, but use sprayers or minisprinklers if your soil is very porous or sandy.

Don't worry if some of the devices you select prove to be inadequate, however. You can make changes or additions once the system is in place.

PLACING THE COMPONENTS

To determine how many drip devices you need for each plant and where to place them, consider the type of soil and the size of the root zone (the horizontal extent of the roots). The devices you select should always water more than 50 percent of the root zone. You can use devices with different flow rates to deliver more water to some plants and less to others on the same circuit. Just be sure to put drip emitters on separate circuits from sprayers and minisprinklers, which require more pressure and put out significantly more water. If you want to maximize the number of drip devices on a single circuit, choose the slowest drip emitters or sprayers and water for a longer period of time.

Mark the devices and their outputs for each area on your garden plan. Note where any pressure-compensating emitters are needed, such as on slopes. Also sketch in lines to connect the watering devices in each circuit to a control valve.

DRIP EMITTER SELECTION GUIDE

This chart provides general guidelines for the number and gallonage of emitters for various types of plantings. Wherever a range is given for the number of emitters, choose the higher number for sandy soil and the lower number for clay soil.

	OUTPUT RATE	NUMBER OF EMITTERS	PLACEMENT
Vegetables (closely spaced)	½–1 gph	1	every 12 inches
Vegetables (widely spaced)	1–2 gph	1	at base of plant
Flower Beds	1 gph	1	at base of plant
Ground Covers	1 gph	1	at base of plant
Shrubs (2–3 ft.)	1 gph	1–2	at base of plant
Shrubs and Trees (3–5 ft.)	1 gph	2	6–12 inches on either side
Shrubs and Trees (5–10 ft.)	2 gph	2–3	2 feet from trunk
Shrubs and Trees (10–20 ft.)	2 gph	3–4	3 feet apart, at drip line
Trees (over 20 ft.)	2 gph	6 or more	4 feet apart, at drip line

SPRAYER SELECTION GUIDE

Many sprayers are adjustable or offer a selection of nozzles, so you're bound to find types that will adequately cover the areas you wish to irrigate. This list is a sampling of typical arcs, radius distances, and output rates.

FULL CIRCLE	HALF CIRCLE	QUARTER CIRCLE	BOW TIE	OUTPUT RATE
8 ft.	5 ft.	5 ft.	4 ft.	6 gph
9 ft.	6 ft.	6 ft.	5 ft.	10 gph
11 ft.	7 ft.	7 ft.	6 ft.	17 gph
12 ft.	8 ft.	8 ft.	7 ft.	24 gph

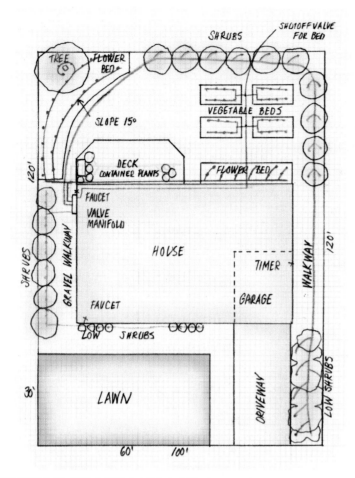

MAXIMUM FLOW RATES FOR DRIP TUBING

For proper operation of your drip system, try to keep within the recommended flow and length limits.

DRIP TUBING

	DIAMETER	MAXIMUM FLOW RATE	MAXIMUM LENGTH
Polyethylene Tubing	½ in.	320 gph	200 ft.
	⅜ in.	100 gph	100 ft.
	¼ in.	15 gph	25 ft.
Heavyweight Vinyl	¼ in.	12 gph	20 ft.

EMITTER LINE (½-GPH EMITTERS)

TUBING DIAMETER	EMITTER SPACING	MAXIMUM LENGTH
½ in.	12 in. apart	200 ft.
½ in.	18 in. apart	260 ft.
½ in.	24 in. apart	320 ft.
¼ in.	6 in. apart	15 ft.
¼ in.	12 in. apart	25 ft.

PUTTING IT ALL TOGETHER

Once you map out your watering devices, you can compute how much tubing and how many fittings you will need. When laying out the main drip line for each circuit, try to connect emitters directly to the line wherever possible. Microtubing serves a purpose, but too much can be a nuisance. It snags rakes and tools and is easier to displace or damage. For drip tubing on a slope, plan to run a main drip line downhill and tee off it with separate horizontal runs of tubing, rather than weaving one line across the hillside.

List the number of devices of each type by output and calculate the total output for each circuit. The chart at left provides a guideline for the maximum flow rate a circuit can handle. If the total output from your watering devices is much less than the maximum, or if you are using pressure-compensating emitters, the tubing can be longer. If it's over the maximum, change to slower devices or use more than one circuit for the hydrozone. For a drip circuit that starts farther out than 200 feet from its control valve, lay PVC pipe underground to the irrigation area and run your drip tubing off a riser. (See pages 48–49 for directions on laying pipe.) Alternatively, run ¾-inch polyethylene tubing aboveground to the start of the new zone and connect ½-inch tubing to it there.

OTHER ESSENTIAL COMPONENTS

To complete your supply list, you'll need several other items. Any drip system needs a backflow preventer (see page 43). Backflow preventers can be located at the point of connection, along the main irrigation line to the control valves, or in the control valves themselves.

As with a sprinkler system, you have a choice of control valves and timers (see pages 10 and 18–19). Drip systems also require head assemblies, one per circuit. A head assembly always includes a filter and a pressure regulator, and may include a fertilizer injector. You assemble it yourself from separate pieces (see page 58). Place a head assembly at the hose bibb for a single drip circuit, or just after each control valve on a multicircuit system. If you connect at the hose bibb, use components with hose threads. To connect to a control valve, you'll need components with pipe threads.

FILTERS Small, in-line filters are the least expensive and are usually fine for small systems and clean water supplies, but you have to take apart the line to wash the screen. Larger Y-filters allow for easy cleaning.

PRESSURE REGULATORS A pressure regulator lowers the household water pressure, which is often too high for a drip system, to a more suitable 15 to 30 psi, protecting the fittings from blowing apart and helping watering devices work properly. Regulators come in a range of psi ratings. Use 25- to 30-psi regulators for most circuits; 20 psi is better for a circuit starting at the top of a slope, since water gains pressure as it travels downhill. Sprayers and minisprinklers with rotors take a higher pressure than drip emitters do; check the manufacturer's information.

You can also place an adjustable brass pressure regulator at the start of the system, before the valves, although it gives you less control of the individual circuits. If your water pressure is very high (over 80 psi), install a pressure regulator both before the valves, to protect them, and in the head assemblies after each valve.

FERTILIZER INJECTORS Drip irrigation does not work well with traditional methods of fertilizing, which rely on overhead watering to dissolve and spread the fertilizer. Consider installing a fertilizer injector, which sends nutrients directly into the plants' water supply.

FERTILIZER INJECTOR

The tools to install a drip system are simple and easy to use. Cut the tubing with a good pair of pruning shears or a utility knife. A specially designed punch makes holes in tubing for emitters and connectors, and "goof plugs" stop up holes in the wrong spots. Stakes hold tubing in place.

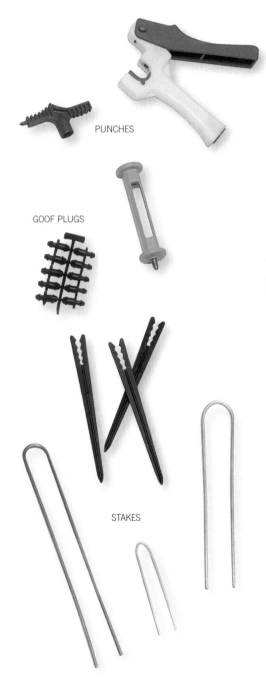

PUNCHES

GOOF PLUGS

STAKES

installing the system

Before doing anything else, separate all the pieces—fittings, drip emitters, sprayers, minisprinklers, misters, bubblers, goof plugs, and stakes—into marked containers or bags. Organize them by size and type so that when you start the installation you won't have to go sifting through a mass of devices to find the one you need.

For a new, stand-alone drip system, identify where you are going to connect the drip system to your water supply and make that connection (see page 42). Drip circuits being added to a sprinkler system merely require their own control valves.

Once you have a place to connect to, prepare a head assembly and position the water distribution lines for one circuit at a time. Flush the lines clear of any debris, then install the watering devices. You can reposition lines and add or subtract drip emitters and sprayers as you go along.

CONSTRUCTING HEAD ASSEMBLIES

A head assembly includes only a few pieces, but it can be bulky enough to be in danger of being knocked into and harmed. Add suitable bracing if you feel it's necessary.

CONNECTING AT THE HOSE BIBB The components for a head assembly at a hose bibb have hose threads that are compatible with the threads on the faucet. Hose-thread parts are lighter than pipe-thread parts and will carry less flow, so be sure that all the watering devices on the circuit combined don't exceed the maximum flow rate for the part.

For a typical faucet connection, first screw on a battery-operated timer, if you choose to use one. Then attach a vacuum breaker, a filter, a pressure regulator, and a thread-to-tubing compression adapter. If you use a fertilizer injector, it goes between the vacuum breaker and the filter. The washers in hose-thread parts should seal properly when the parts are hand-tightened; don't use a wrench.

CONNECTING AT THE CONTROL VALVE Head assemblies on a multicircuit system connect to the control valves and are made of components with pipe threads. Wrap the threads with pipe-thread tape before hand-tightening (you can use a wrench, but do so gently). Be sure to assemble the parts with the arrows pointing in the direction of water flow.

Screw the components together, starting with the filter and then the pressure regulator. Make sure to use the correct psi-rated regulator for a given circuit. After the pressure regulator, attach a thread-to-tubing adapter. If you opt for a fertilizer injector, install it between the valve and the filter.

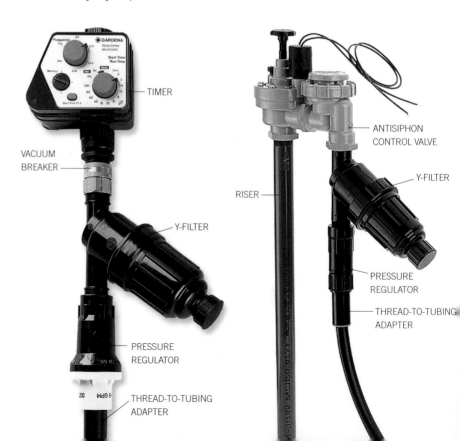

TIMER

VACUUM BREAKER

Y-FILTER

PRESSURE REGULATOR

THREAD-TO-TUBING ADAPTER

ANTISIPHON CONTROL VALVE

RISER

Y-FILTER

PRESSURE REGULATOR

THREAD-TO-TUBING ADAPTER

LAYING THE DRIP TUBING

Drip tubing is easy to install. Start by inserting the drip tubing into the thread-to-tubing adapter at the end of the head assembly. Lay the tubing for the whole circuit, following your irrigation layout. To avoid kinking the tubing, unroll it as you lay it out, rather than pulling it out of a coil lying on the ground. Leave a little slack for adjustments and anchor it to the ground with stakes at intervals. Try to keep dirt out of the tubing as you work.

If you need to run drip tubing under a walkway, use the method described on page 45. To make acute turns, cut the tubing with pruning shears and rejoin the ends with an elbow. To branch the line, cut it and rejoin the pieces in the arms of a tee; insert additional drip hose or emitter line in the stem of the tee.

Emitter line can be laid either at the same time as the tubing or when you install the emitters and sprayers.

Polyethylene tubing can be stiff when it is cold. In a warm climate, take it outdoors early and leave it in the sun to soften. If you have trouble inserting the tubing into a fitting, dip the end into hot water to soften it more. Do not use soap or any lubricant, such as grease or oil, to force the tubing in. Never force the tubing too far into a compression fitting or it may interfere with the water flow; an inch into the fitting should be enough.

Drip line is unrolled as it is laid out to keep it from kinking.

59

RANDOM PLANTINGS IN BEDS When plants are randomly spaced, run $\frac{1}{2}$-inch tubing through the bed so that it passes as many plants as possible. If a circuit covers just one planting bed, a good technique is to create a spiral around the area, starting with the plants on the outside of the bed and spiraling the tubing into the center. Another option is to run the tubing in a snake pattern through the bed and send $\frac{1}{4}$-inch microtubing off the main drip line to individual plants farther away.

STRAIGHT ROWS AND VEGETABLE BEDS The most efficient way to irrigate long rows of plants with drip is to run parallel lines of $\frac{1}{4}$-inch or $\frac{1}{2}$-inch emitter line along the row of plants. Tee off the lines from the main drip line. You can also use drip tubing with emitters rather than emitter line.

ABOVE: Randomly spaced plants are watered by $\frac{1}{2}$-inch emitter line that snakes through this front flower bed.

BELOW LEFT: A vegetable bed will be evenly watered by parallel lines of $\frac{1}{4}$-inch emitter line teed off from a $\frac{1}{2}$-inch main drip line.

BELOW RIGHT: When installing raised flower or vegetable beds, run drip tubing under the frame and up into each bed to keep it out of sight. The main line can be hidden with a layer of mulch.

A mister is suspended above a hanging plant and kept in place with a spiral of thin wire.

CONTAINER PLANTS Container plants require their own circuit because they need to be watered more frequently—as much as once or twice a day in hot weather. First run a ³⁄₈-inch or ¹⁄₂-inch main drip line from your head assembly to the container area; you can hide it along a wall or walkway, or even under a deck. Although ³⁄₈-inch tubing is less noticeable, it should not be run farther than 100 feet.

Next, tee off the main drip line to run ¹⁄₄-inch microtubing to the pots. You can run it over the lip of the pot (using an elbow will keep it flat) or up through the drainage hole. Depending on the container and the plant, the microtubing can connect to one or more drip emitters, to a ¹⁄₄-inch emitter line, or to a small bubbler, sprayer, or mister. Use

heavyweight vinyl tubing instead of polyethylene. It will hug the contours of the container and turn corners without elbows or other fittings. It also comes in several colors to blend with the container color.

For hanging baskets, run microtubing up posts, under eaves, or in the joint between two walls. To prevent backflow on hanging baskets, leave at least 2 inches between the drip emitters or misters and the foliage or soil.

BELOW LEFT: A length of ¹⁄₄-inch emitter line wraps around the root zone of a container plant. The main drip line runs along a nearby wall. BELOW RIGHT: Two emitters deliver water to opposite sides of a container with the use of a tee fitting at the end of the microtubing.

END CAP

FIGURE-EIGHT
CLOSURE

SELF-FLUSHING
END CAP

INSTALLING WATERING DEVICES

Before you add watering devices to the tubing, flush it free of dirt and debris. Once the water runs clear from the ends of the lines, turn off the water and close the lines with end caps or figure-eight closures. Figure-eights are simple to install but are less easily removed when flushing the line. End caps come in both compression and locking styles and have a tip that can be unscrewed to flush the line; some are designed to flush automatically before and after each watering period.

Use your irrigation layout as a guide in locating the various watering devices, but rely on your own judgment in repositioning them as needed.

DRIP EMITTERS To install a drip emitter directly into ½- or ³⁄₈-inch drip tubing, punch a hole in the tubing (sidebar, opposite) and then insert the barbed end of the emitter. You can also install an emitter on microtubing run from the main drip line. Connect one end of the microtubing to a hole in the drip line with a barbed ¼-inch connector. Then insert an emitter into the other end and position it at the plant. You can hold the emitter in place with a stake. On slopes, locate emitters on the uphill side of the plant.

To make a chain of in-line emitters, string them together with microtubing, then secure the microtubing to the main drip line with a barbed connector. The microtubing coming from the water source goes into the colored side of the emitter. Use a goof plug or emitter to cap the end of the microtubing.

BELOW LEFT: A run of microtubing is attached to the larger drip tubing. BELOW RIGHT: Staking a drip emitter on the end of a run of microtubing keeps it exactly where you want it. OPPOSITE PAGE, BOTTOM: A drip sprayer covers a small planting area without wasting water.

SPRAYERS, MINISPRINKLERS, AND MISTERS To install a spray device, run microtubing from a hole in the main drip line, attaching it with a barbed connector. Extend the microtubing to a plastic stake at the desired location. Some devices screw directly to the stake; otherwise, the stake merely supports the microtubing. Pop-up sprayers and minisprinklers go into the ground. Some come with optional protector attachments to keep soil out. Some mister heads come with built-in spikes as well as barbed connectors that can attach directly to a main drip line or microtubing.

EMITTER LINE Larger, ½-inch emitter line can be connected to the main drip line with a compression fitting such as a tee, an elbow, or a coupling. Plug the end with an end cap. Attach ¼-inch emitter line to the drip line with a barbed connector and seal the end with a goof plug or, if you want extra flushing action, a drip emitter.

HOLE PUNCH POINTERS

When making holes in drip tubing for emitters and barbed fittings, use a punch designed for the purpose. Make sure the tubing is lying straight and in its final orientation, not twisted. Position the hole so that the emitter will drip to the side or downward. Hold the punch at a right angle to the tubing to ensure a round hole that will seal tightly against the emitter's barb. You may find the piercing process to be easier if you slowly twist the punch as you push it into the tubing. On some punches, the tip may become clogged; clear it out before punching again. If you punch a hole in the wrong place, seal it with a goof plug.

FINISHING THE INSTALLATION

The last step in installing drip irrigation is to test the system. If you haven't connected your drip control valves to the timer, do so now (see page 47). Open the shutoff valve and then switch on each circuit manually at the timer. If none of the circuits comes on, inspect the control valves to be sure they were installed in the right direction, and check the wiring at the valves and the controller. If only one circuit fails to come on, check the flow-control setting at that valve.

Once the water is flowing, look for leaks. If you left any open holes in the tubing, fill them with goof plugs. If tubing has been accidentally gashed, cut out that piece and put in a compression coupling.

Next, check for clogged emitters and sprayers and clean them out (see page 80). Make sure all the watering devices are positioned near plants; if necessary, move them and plug holes in the tubing. Adjust the direction or throw of the sprayers and mini-sprinklers as required.

When everything is working properly, you can cover the tubing with mulch.

During your final check of the system, look for water spraying from a hole that was placed mistakenly or is no longer meant to be used. You can easily seal such holes with goof plugs once you spot them.

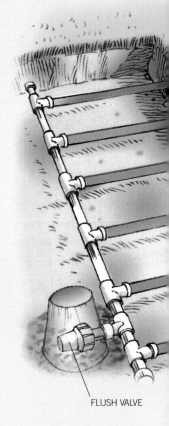

FLUSH VALVE

Drip irrigation usually involves tubing laid on top of your soil, but it can also be installed belowground for some purposes. One such application is for watering lawns, for which emitter line is used. A special emitter line is available with a slow-release herbicide mixed into the plastic of each emitter to keep out roots.

Where appropriate, a subsurface drip system offers several advantages. The primary benefit is water conservation, because no moisture is lost to evaporation, runoff, or overspray. Subsurface emitter line also delivers

SUBSURFACE DRIP FOR LAWNS

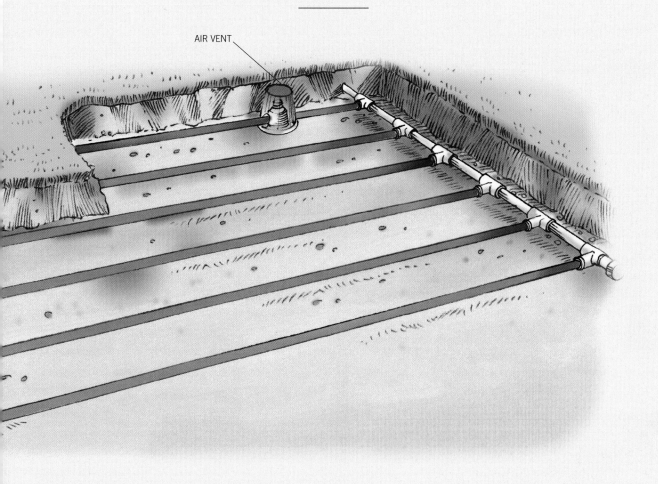

AIR VENT

water more uniformly, resulting in a healthier lawn. Weeds don't grow as readily because there is no surface moisture to encourage their spread, and the system also cuts down on turf diseases.

Subsurface drip isn't the answer for every lawn, however. It's ideal for lawns that are hard to water efficiently with sprinklers, such as those with narrow strips, steep slopes, and odd shapes. It's not as well suited for large areas or for an area with many tree roots. And it's a risk in areas with gophers or moles, which may chew through the tubing.

The basic design consists of parallel emitter lines placed about 4 to 6 inches below the soil. In an existing lawn, dig trenches as described on pages 44–45. If you are laying down a new lawn, install the system before the final 4 inches of soil is spread.

In loose, sandy soils, use emitter line with emitters spaced 12 inches apart and place the lines as close as 12 inches apart. In heavy, clay soils, use emitter line with emitters spaced 18 inches apart and place the lines 18 inches apart. On a slope, the lines should be about 25 percent closer together than normal at the top and 25 percent farther apart toward the bottom. To prevent dry strips, place lines no more than 4 inches from walkways or other hard edges.

Connect the parallel emitter lines with PVC headers at both ends. At the header farthest from the water supply, add an automatic flush valve in a protective valve box. The valve operates briefly whenever the system shuts down, flushing debris from the tubing. Also install an air vent at the highest point of the layout. The air vent operates as the flush valve is draining; by allowing air to replace water in the tubing, it helps prevent suction of sediment into the emitters. Place the air vent in a valve box with good drainage.

converting to drip

There are several good reasons to convert all or part of an old sprinkler system to drip irrigation. For example, you may find that plants in front of some of the sprinkler heads have grown and are blocking the spray from reaching other plants. Or, your household water pressure or flow rate may have been reduced or old galvanized pipes may have corroded, keeping your sprinkler system from carrying enough water to the sprinkler heads. Or you may now be finding that wind or other conditions make drip a more efficient watering system. Happily, sprinkler circuits can be readily converted to a drip system. With the addition of the right components, the underground sprinkler pipes will deliver the water to drip tubing on the surface.

FULL DRIP CONVERSION

To convert an entire sprinkler circuit to drip, work on one circuit at a time, using either of the methods described below. Begin by removing all the sprinkler heads from the risers. Be sure to flush the old sprinkler line before new components are added. After you have finished the conversion and before using the converted circuit for the first time, leave the end caps off all the drip tubing and flush the tubes for a few minutes. Cap all the risers you don't use.

One conversion method is to connect a PVC swivel fitting (an elbow or a tee) to one or more risers, adding compression adapters that accept ½-inch drip tubing or emitter line. From there, attach drip watering devices as with any drip circuit. If you use this approach, you'll need to add a head assembly (see page 58) at the beginning of the system, just after the control valve, or after the backflow protector in a single-circuit system. An expandable PVC coupling reconnects the assembly to the pipe.

Another option is handy if you only need to run a few lines of drip tubing around the area covered by the old sprinkler circuit.

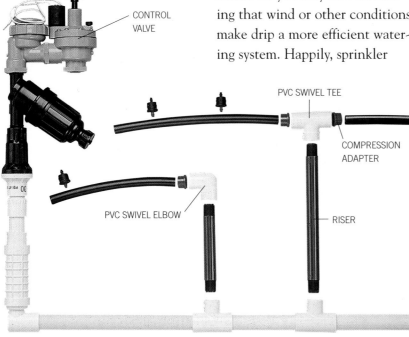

CONTROL VALVE

PVC SWIVEL TEE

COMPRESSION ADAPTER

PVC SWIVEL ELBOW

RISER

ABOVE: A sprinkler circuit can be converted to drip irrigation by adding a new head assembly to the start of the circuit and running ½-inch drip tubing from each riser (connect the riser to the tubing with a PVC swivel fitting). BELOW: If you dedicate an entire circuit to drip but use only a few risers, you can install a sprinkler body replacement like this one on each riser you use; it comes with a built-in filter and pressure regulator.

RETROFIT SPRINKLER BODY

In essence, you can add a head assembly right at each riser you use—remove the sprinkler head, attach a PVC elbow, and install a Y-filter and pressure regulator. Be sure to cap any unused risers. An even simpler variation on this method is to install a retrofit sprinkler body replacement that comes with a built-in filter and pressure regulator (opposite, bottom). Either approach can be expensive, though, if you apply it to more than just one or two sprinkler heads.

PARTIAL CONVERSION

If you want to keep most of your sprinkler heads on a given circuit running but wish to convert just one or two to drip, you can screw multioutlet emitters directly onto one or more risers in the circuit. This solution is most effective when you have only a few plants or shrubs close to an existing sprinkler head that is not in use.

A multioutlet emitter has a built-in filter and flow controls, ranging from 5 to 20 gph. Multioutlet emitters can have as few as 2 outlets or as many as 12, each with a barbed insert for microtubing. Each outlet is designed to send water to the open end of the microtubing, or to a drip sprayer whose flow requirement must be carefully matched to the output of the device. Multioutlet emitters can deliver a useful amount of water in the short run time that's typical of lawn sprinklers. The disadvantage of this method is the large amount of microtubing needed, which can be unattractive and increases maintenance.

An ineffective sprinkler circuit can become an efficient irrigation system when it's converted to drip.

Multioutlet emitters are handy for converting one or two risers on a sprinkler circuit to drip irrigation; other risers on the circuit are still used for standard sprinkler heads.

8-OUTLET EMITTER

4-OUTLET EMITTER

OPERATING MANUAL

With your irrigation system installed, your challenge now is learning how to use it and maintain it. An automated system relieves you of a lot of work, but you still have to program the timer, reassess the watering schedule as the seasons change, and keep the system in good working order.

Formulas exist for calculating watering needs based on the rate at which water is depleted from the soil, but this chapter suggests much simpler methods for establishing a watering schedule. With these techniques you can provide your plants with the right amount of water and create a schedule that works in your garden.

This chapter also provides a maintenance guide and help with troubleshooting problems you might encounter once your system is installed and running. The final pages include instructions for making simple repairs.

establishing a schedule

The simplest strategy for creating a watering schedule is to water to the depth of a plant's root zone and then apply more water when the root zone becomes almost dry. See the illustration below for general depth guidelines. To minimize water loss from evaporation, especially if you're running sprinklers, water early in the morning before the sun is most intense and while the air is relatively calm. Between 3:00 A.M. and 6:00 A.M. is considered ideal. Try to set the timer to end before your indoor water use begins for the day.

HOW MUCH IS ENOUGH?

Soil absorption and evaporation rates vary between gardens and even within them. To determine the right amount of water for your plants, work with each zone in your garden separately. Turn on the water for a set amount of time. Then, use a soil probe (or, for containers, a moisture meter) to determine how deeply the water has penetrated. A soil probe that extracts a core of soil literally shows you the level of moisture belowground.

An 18-inch-long soil probe is sufficient for most plantings; one

model has holes at 2-inch intervals that enable you to quickly gauge moisture penetration and root depth. You can also use any long metal rod to estimate moisture depth; it will move easily through wet soil and stop or become harder to push when it hits dry soil. Moisture meters sold for home use typically have a short probe attached to a dial that shows relative wetness or dryness. Home models will stand up to use in potting

SOIL PROBE

To water to a plant's root depth, use the depth guidelines illustrated here. If you're using a drip system, also keep in mind the width of the plants' root zones. In a mature plant it may extend from 1½ times (in clay soils) to 3 times (in loose soils) the diameter of the plant's foliage or crown.

COMPARATIVE ROOT DEPTHS

6 IN.
12 IN.
18 IN.
24 IN.

soils, but the probe is usually too short to gauge the moisture level of established, inground plants.

Adjust the watering time based on what you observe. For instance, if the probe shows the ground is moist only to a depth of 2 inches yet the root depth should be 6 inches, you need to water about 3 times as long. If necessary, turn on the water again and take another sample, repeating the process until the water reaches the appropriate depth. Note the length of time it took to water the zone.

If the water runs off before it penetrates deep enough, try pulse irrigation. Water in short cycles, stopping to allow the soil to absorb the water, then repeating. To determine an effective pulse irrigation schedule, shut off the water each time you see it begin to run off. Test the soil for wetness and determine how much longer you need to water. Wait until all moisture has soaked into the soil and then turn the water back on for another interval, just short of the length of time it took for runoff to occur. Repeat these on-off cycles until the entire root zone is moist. Note the length and number of cycles for each zone.

WATERING FREQUENCY

After you've tested how much to water, use your soil probe every day to check the soil's moisture level. For all but moisture-loving plants, if the soil sample is dry

on top but moist where the roots are growing, hold off on watering. If the entire root zone is barely dry, it's time to water. For moisture-loving plants, water again when the soil is still a bit moist. Again, keep a record of the plants' requirements.

You now have the information you need to program your timer to irrigate all your zones automatically. Retest the soil moisture level periodically to make sure the schedule is effective.

SEASONAL ADJUSTMENT Be prepared to make adjustments to your watering schedule as the weather and seasons change. Water more often during very hot, dry, or windy weather. When it's cool or humid, less frequent watering is in order. In winter, when the days are short and the sun is low and less intense, even nondormant plants demand much less water than they do in the summer. If you have a rain sensor attached to your timer, it will automatically turn the system off during rainy periods (see page 19). If not, remember to turn it off by hand. A rain gauge will tell you how much rain has fallen so you can estimate when to turn the system back on.

TOP: An inexpensive moisture meter provides an easy way to test the soil around shallow-rooted seedlings for moisture. BOTTOM: A rain gauge lets you know if enough rain has fallen to replace a full watering by your irrigation system. If so, temporarily turn off your controller.

maintaining the system

Whether you've installed a sprinkler or a drip system or a hybrid that combines the two, you need to monitor your system regularly to make sure it is operating efficiently. Maintenance falls into three categories: the type needed at the beginning of the growing season, ongoing upkeep and adaptations during the season, and preparing the system for winter.

SEASONAL CHECKLIST

At the start of every season, turn on the water for each circuit and check the lines and watering devices for leaks, blockages, or broken parts. Water-filled valve boxes or leaking sprinkler heads may be a sign that valves need to be repaired or replaced. If you find any problems, refer to pages 76–81 for help in fixing them.

FLUSHING THE SYSTEM At least once a year for sprinkler systems and every 6 months for drip systems, flush the lines to minimize clogging from loose debris. If you are using water that may contain sediment, flush a drip system more frequently.

For sprinkler systems, remove the spray nozzle or rotor at the end of each line of pipe and turn on the water for several minutes until it runs clear from the risers. For drip circuits, open all end caps and run the water for 2 to 5 minutes.

If your water source is well, pond, or gray water, algae can build up. To eliminate it, flush the system with granular chlorine (not liquid chlorine, which may harm plants) or another product made for that purpose.

CLEANING FILTERS The filters in a drip system, and the small filters below spray nozzles in a sprinkler system, should be cleaned frequently. (Brass spray heads may need cleaning more often because they lack filters.) If you have a clean municipal water supply, once a year may suffice. To clean an in-line filter, remove its screen and wash it under running water; replace any screen that is damaged. A Y- or T-filter can be cleaned out by unscrewing the cap and removing the filter. Some have flush valves that allow you to clean the screen in place.

TOP: When water flushes freely from the end of drip tubing, you know it is free of debris that can cause the emitters to clog. BOTTOM: Most filters can be flushed by opening a flush valve or removing an end cap from the bottom of the filter.

INSPECTING WATERING DEVICES

It's best to inspect your system at regular intervals, at the hour when it is normally in use. Turn each circuit on in sequence. Once the circuit is on, observe the sprinkler heads in a sprinkler system, or the watering devices in a drip irrigation system.

If the spray of any sprinkler head is off center, turn the head or nozzle or adjust the arc. If water shoots straight up from a sprinkler riser, it is likely that the riser has been damaged or the spray head or rotor has been broken off; replace the damaged piece. If all the sprinklers in a zone are underperforming, the water pressure may have dropped. Check for a partially closed valve, a misadjustment to the main pressure regulator, a sprinkler valve that is not opening fully, or an underground pipe leak (see below). If spray or rotor nozzles or drip devices fail to put out a steady spray or stream, they may be clogged and should be cleared. If you can't clear a clogged watering device, install a new one.

INSPECTING PIPES AND TUBING

It is easier to find and repair leaks in drip tubing aboveground than in PVC pipes belowground. Puddles, miniature geysers, and eroded soil are clues. If you see those, inspect the tubing around them until you find the damage. Small leaks in drip tubing will appear as spraying or bubbling along the line.

LEFT: If a sprinkler head breaks off from its riser, water shoots up in a geyser when the system is turned on. RIGHT: Water will only dribble from a clogged sprinkler head and be wasted.

A dead or dried-out plant is a telltale sign of a clogged emitter.

Often the only sign of a leak in an underground pipe is an unexpected rise in your water bill. Another sign may be a swampy area of ground that won't dry out. If you suspect an underground leak, cap off all the sprinkler heads in each circuit, then turn on the water. Wait for a puddle to appear on the surface. Dig carefully to expose the break or crack in the pipe; careless digging could cause additional cracks. Repair the pipe as shown on page 80.

ADAPTING THE SYSTEM

As plants grow or as you add plantings to your landscape, you may need to add or move sprinkler heads or drip devices. At the beginning of each growing season and at regular intervals, check to see whether the output from any of your watering devices is blocked by other plants. If that's the case, either cut back the foliage or alter the height or position of the device. In the case of sprinkler heads, you may need to replace the riser with a longer one or add a riser extension, unless you have an adjustable riser.

If you've increased the size of your garden, you can add new risers and sprinkler heads to a sprinkler circuit or watering devices to a drip circuit as long as you've left room for growth. If the existing circuits can't handle more output, or the devices you want to add don't have the same flow rates as those already installed, you'll need to add a new circuit to the system.

ADDING SPRINKLER RISERS You can add new risers to an existing circuit in two ways: either along an existing line of PVC pipe or on a new line you branch off from an old line. When you add a branch to a circuit, refer to the routing recommendations on page 40. The steps at right show how to add a riser to an existing line.

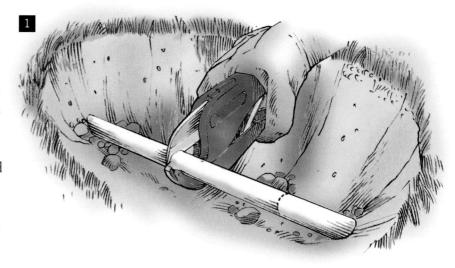

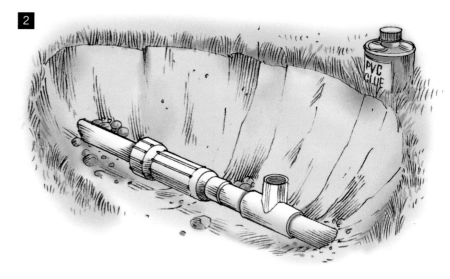

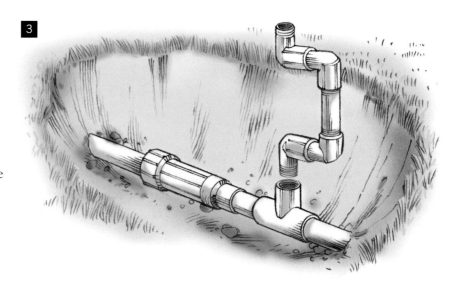

1 Cut pipe

Locate the spot where you want to add a riser. Dig very carefully down to the pipe, making a hole wide and deep enough to work with the pipe easily without getting soil into the system. Using PVC ratcheting cutters, cut out a section of the PVC pipe wide enough to insert an adjustable slip-fix coupling and a tee fitting with a threaded outlet for the riser.

2 Install fittings

Cement the slip-fix to one cut end of pipe and the tee to the other. Adjust the fittings to fit the space as necessary. Make sure to plan ahead so that the tee is facing straight up; remember that solvent cement dries very fast.

3 Attach the riser

Using the appropriate height and type of riser for the location, wrap the riser threads with pipe-thread tape and screw the riser into the tee fitting.

WINTERIZING THE SYSTEM

If you live in a cold-winter climate, drain your irrigation system prior to the first freeze before water can freeze in the pipes and cause them to burst. First, close the system's shut-off valve.

In a sprinkler system, most of the water in the underground pipes will already have drained out if you installed automatic drain valves at the low points in the system (see page 48). Manually open each of the control valves to release pressure in the pipes. The best way to remove any remaining water from the system is to blow compressed air through it—this is usually a job for a professional.

In a drip system, remove or open the end closures to allow the lines to drain. Unscrew any head assemblies and drain any Y- or T-filters. Bring the head assemblies indoors. You can leave the drip lines in place once you have drained them and left the ends open. Bury the lines under heavy mulch for the winter to protect them.

In milder climates where occasional frost occurs, wrap any aboveground pipes or valves that will contain water with foam tubing or insulating tape.

Be sure to flush the lines before using the system again in the spring.

In any climate where occasional frost is possible, wrap aboveground pipes with insulating foam tubing or tape.

simple repairs

Most of the repairs you'll need to do for either underground sprinkler or drip systems follow the same techniques used to install your pipes, tubing, and watering devices. If you installed your irrigation system yourself, you'll be familiar with its components and how they work together. If you didn't, a quick review of the previous chapters will help. The following pages provide a quick guide to trouble-shooting and making simple repairs.

CAP

O-RING

SEAT WASHE

BONNET

DIAPHRAGM
ASSEMBLY

SOLENOID

Simple repairs and maintenance will keep your irrigation system at its best.

CLEANING VALVES

The best way to keep your control valves in good shape is to inspect and clean them regularly, especially if you are using hard water or well water that is high in sediment. Dirt and debris caught in a valve can cause it to drip, producing a permanent puddle at the lowest sprinkler head or drip device.

If you suspect the valve has a damaged part or some debris in it, turn off the water supply and

A control valve is easy to take apart and inspect. If the diaphragm is damaged, replace it. If you can't find damage or debris but the valve does not operate properly, it is best to install a new valve.

remove the bonnet. Inspect and clean the seat washer and seat, remove the diaphragm, and flush the valve with water to clean out any dirt or debris. If the valve is stuck, inspect the diaphragm for tears or holes. If it's damaged, replace it with a new one. Reseat the diaphragm and replace the bonnet. Make sure the outlet port (out of which the water flows) is clear and unclogged.

TROUBLESHOOTING GUIDE

If you check and maintain your irrigation system regularly, you should experience few problems with it. When problems do occur, consult this guide.

APPARATUS	PROBLEM	POSSIBLE SOLUTIONS
Timers and Valves	System doesn't come on	Check whether timer is turned on. Check for blown fuse; replace if necessary. Check if programming is off; reset timer. Check for and repair faulty wiring.
	Watering cycle repeats	Check program; eliminate extra start times.
	Fuses blow	Check for and replace faulty valve solenoid. Check for and repair faulty wiring.
	One circuit doesn't work	Check for and repair faulty wiring at the timer or control valve. Also see solutions for "control valve won't open."
	Control valve won't close	Clean out debris inside control valve (see page 76). Check for and replace damaged or worn seat, washer, or diaphragm. Lower the flow-control setting.
	Control valve won't open	Open the flow control. Unclog outlet port. Check for and replace burned-out solenoid. Check for and repair faulty wiring at the timer or control valve.
Sprinkler System	Misdirected spray	Adjust spray (see page 78). Unclog sprinkler head (see page 78).
	Sprinkler won't pop up	Open control valve all the way. Water pressure may be insufficient; break circuit into two, or convert circuit to drip (see pages 66–67).
	Sprinkler won't retract	Check for and replace damaged sprinkler head (see page 50), or replace cap and the wiper seal through which the pop-up section rises.
	Water spurting from sprinkler body	Check for missing nozzle and replace if needed. Check for broken sprinkler head or riser and replace (see page 50 for sprinkler head, page 79 for riser).
	Water dribbles from nozzle	Clear out debris from nozzle and internal filter (see page 78). Check for broken underground pipe and repair with coupling (see page 80).
	Rotor does not rotate or rotates in only one direction	Clear debris from rotor nozzle (see page 78) or from stator, the part that delivers water to the base of the turbine. Check for missing nozzle and replace if needed. Water pressure may be insufficient; break circuit into two or convert circuit to drip (see pages 66–67).
	Swampy area in garden	Check for broken underground pipe and repair with coupling (see page 80).
Drip System	Water dribbles from drip emitter or spray	Clear debris from device (see page 80).
	No water coming out of emitters	Check for and correct kinks in drip tubing. Flush system to remove debris (see page 72). Remove emitter to check pressure in tubing.
	Emitters pop out frequently	Water pressure is too high; replace pressure regulator with lower-pressure version.
	Puddle in garden	Check for and repair tears or holes in tubing (see page 81); check that valve is closing completely.

The flow rate of many spray heads can be easily adjusted with a small screwdriver. Others require a special tool provided by the manufacturer.

SIMPLE SPRINKLER REPAIRS

While sprinkler system damage is relatively rare, it does happen. Fixing sprinkler heads is easy; replacing a broken riser requires a little more work, as does repairing pipes, if you are unlucky enough to have one break underground. Most PVC pipe repairs use the same techniques as those for installing the pipe system (see pages 48–49). Use the following instructions to repair the most common problems with sprinkler systems.

ADJUSTING SPRAYS When a spray head or a rotor is misdirected, it is easy to adjust it. With some spray nozzles, you simply turn the head or nozzle to point in the correct direction. With others, you'll need to turn a flow-adjustment screw on the top of the nozzle; use a small screwdriver. Most gear-driven rotors come with a set of nozzles to allow easy adjustment of the throw distance and precipitation rate. If the spray arc is too high or too low, change it with a special tool provided by the manufacturer, following the manufacturer's directions.

CLEANING CLOGGED SPRINKLERS

A clogged sprinkler head will usually force water out at an odd angle, or the spray may be greatly reduced. Any head can become clogged if soil, mineral deposits, insects, or other debris collects in the slits or holes from which the water emerges.

Clean the slits or holes with a piece of thin, stiff wire, such as a straightened paper clip. A dental pick also does the job nicely. With spray heads, if necessary, remove each nozzle according to the manufacturer's directions and hold the nozzle under running water to blast out the debris. Also rinse out the filter basket below the nozzle.

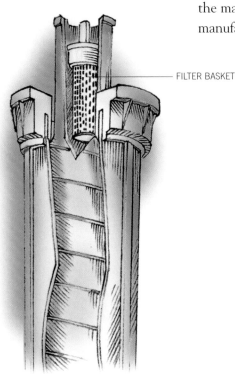

FILTER BASKET

Use an unbent paper clip or other small piece of thin wire to unclog the nozzle of a sprinkler head.

REPLACING A BROKEN RISER

A threaded riser, when damaged, can be replaced by digging around it to the PVC pipe, unscrewing it from its tee fitting, and screwing in a new one. A broken riser may be difficult to extract; use a stub wrench for additional leverage. Put the stub wrench into the riser and twist counterclockwise.

STUB WRENCH

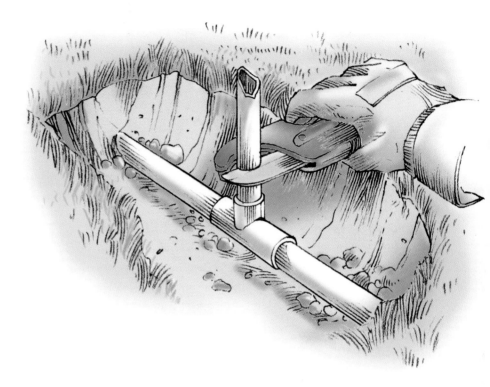

If a nonthreaded riser breaks, replace all or part of it with a threaded riser. If the bottom portion is intact, cut the riser pipe off cleanly a few inches above the tee (right). Cement a slip-threaded coupling to the end of the cut riser. Cut a new threaded riser to length. Wait half an hour, then wrap the riser threads with pipe-thread tape and screw the riser into the tee.

If an entire unthreaded riser is broken, dig a trench around the tee below it, cut out the old tee, and replace it with a new threaded tee (see pages 74–75). Then wait half an hour, wrap the riser threads with pipe-thread tape, and screw in the new riser.

As you work, be careful not to let soil spill into the pipes. After completing the repair, remove all downstream sprinkler heads on the circuit and flush the system until the water runs clear. Then replace the sprinkler heads.

A cracked underground pipe can be repaired with a slip-fix coupling and slip coupling.

Once attached to the old pipe, the slip-fix coupling is adjusted to fit the space.

REPAIRING A LEAK IN PVC PIPE

A minor leak in an underground system can usually be traced to one crack or break in a pipe. Once exposed, the broken section can be cut out and replaced with a slip-fix coupling, as shown above.

Before installing the slip-fix coupling, make sure the water supply is off. Digging carefully to avoid further damage to the pipe, make a trench wide enough and deep enough to work with the pipe easily without getting soil into the system. Clean the pipe next to the area to be mended. Cut out the damaged section with PVC ratcheting cutters, then install the coupling. Adjust it to fit the space as necessary. Flush the system thoroughly and test for leaks before reburying the pipe.

A paper clip makes the perfect tool for unclogging drip emitters.

SIMPLE DRIP SYSTEM REPAIRS

Drip irrigation systems are subject to more damage than sprinkler systems because all their parts are aboveground. Although drip watering devices clog more easily and tubing can be cut or chewed by animals, most of the damage is easy to repair and requires no special tools.

CLOGGED OR BROKEN DRIP DEVICES

If water is dribbling out of a drip watering device at an erratic rate, chances are it is clogged with debris. Use a thin piece of wire (a paper clip does the trick) and run it gently around the inside of the opening of the emitter or spray nozzle. If you can't clear the clog, just replace the device with a new one. Drip watering devices are inexpensive; keep an assortment of them handy for such quick fixes.

SEALING HOLES If you punch a hole in a drip tube by mistake or just need to move an emitter from one location along the tubing to another, fill the hole with a goof plug. Simply push the barbed goof plug into the hole. Keep a bag of extra goof plugs handy for these repairs.

RIGHT: A goof plug seals an unwanted hole in ½-inch drip tubing.

REPAIRING A CUT IN TUBING
A gash in a run of drip tubing can easily be repaired by making clean cuts on either side of the gash and connecting the two cut ends with a coupler.

To join two ends of ½-inch tubing, push each end into a compression coupler. If working with compression fittings is difficult for you, use a locking fitting that requires no force. Insert the tubing into the fitting and turn a locking mechanism at the end of the fitting. For microtubing, connect the two ends with a barbed coupler. Whenever you repair a cut in drip tubing, remove the end caps from the line and flush the system of any dirt or debris that may have gotten inside. Secure any tubing that has gotten loose from its stake.

LEFT: To join two sections of drip tubing, first push one end of tubing into a compression coupling. Then insert the other end.

CHAPTER SIX

A GALLERY OF PLANS

On the following pages you'll find photos of a range of gardens with accompanying layouts by a professional irrigation consultant. They include a wide variety of landscapes—an urban garden with a small lawn and flower beds; a large suburban front lawn and border garden; a sloping hillside of drought-tolerant perennials; a Japanese-influenced entry area; and a well-stocked country garden. But you'll find that the basic principles described in this book apply to each one.

Every garden, including your own, has its own unique set of irrigation requirements, depending on its size and the variety of planting areas and microclimates within it. By using the examples shown here, however, you may find good solutions for individual kinds of planting areas that you can adapt for your own landscape.

The plans shown here suggest an efficient watering solution for each sample garden. Keep in mind, though, that there is often more than one way to water a particular area. For a more detailed explanation of how to determine the watering needs of your plants, see chapter 2.

a small urban oasis

This city garden enjoys full midday sun, flat terrain, and consistent soil quality throughout its planting areas. But a variety of plant locations—lawn, garden beds, and containers—and cut-out shapes around the lawn present real irrigation challenges.

To irrigate each area efficiently, the consultant's plan calls for installing four circuits, two for a drip system and two for a sprinkler system. The rear lawn is small enough to be watered by 12- to 15-foot spray heads. The side lawn can be covered easily with strip spray heads.

Since container plants need to be watered frequently, they have their own drip circuit (purple). The main line of ½-inch drip tubing can be unobtrusively tacked along the side of the house. Spirals of ¼-inch emitter line water the pots.

A second drip circuit (blue) supplies water to the rear-garden beds and shrubs. Buried PVC pipes run under the lawn to the edge of each bed, where risers attach to ½-inch drip tubing. Parallel lines of ¼-inch emitter line then water the rear beds. At the side of the house, individual emitters water the shrubs.

HOUSE

LEGEND

● DRIP CIRCUIT FOR CONTAINER PLANTS

● SPRINKLER CIRCUIT: SPRAY HEADS

● DRIP CIRCUIT FOR IN-GROUND PLANTS

● SPRINKLER CIRCUIT: SPRAY AND STRIP SPRAY HEADS

a grand front garden

Keeping a large, beautifully landscaped front yard looking great is no small feat. With so much space to take care of, our consultant recommends the installation of a low-maintenance underground sprinkler system with a combination of spray heads for the garden beds and rotors for the wide open spaces.

In the illustration, similar types of sprinkler heads are zoned together; the actual number of circuits may vary from this plan and would be determined after testing on-site. Rotors (shown in blues and greens) water the lawn and the garden beds along the sidewalk. Pop-up spray heads along the walkway (purple) are adjusted to cover the lawn and garden bed but avoid wetting the trunk of the old elm tree.

Those spray heads located near the house (shown in orange, yellow, and rose) are placed on fixed risers or 12-inch pop-ups to keep the spray above the plants. The pattern of the spray nozzle used in each spray head is determined by its location in the landscape.

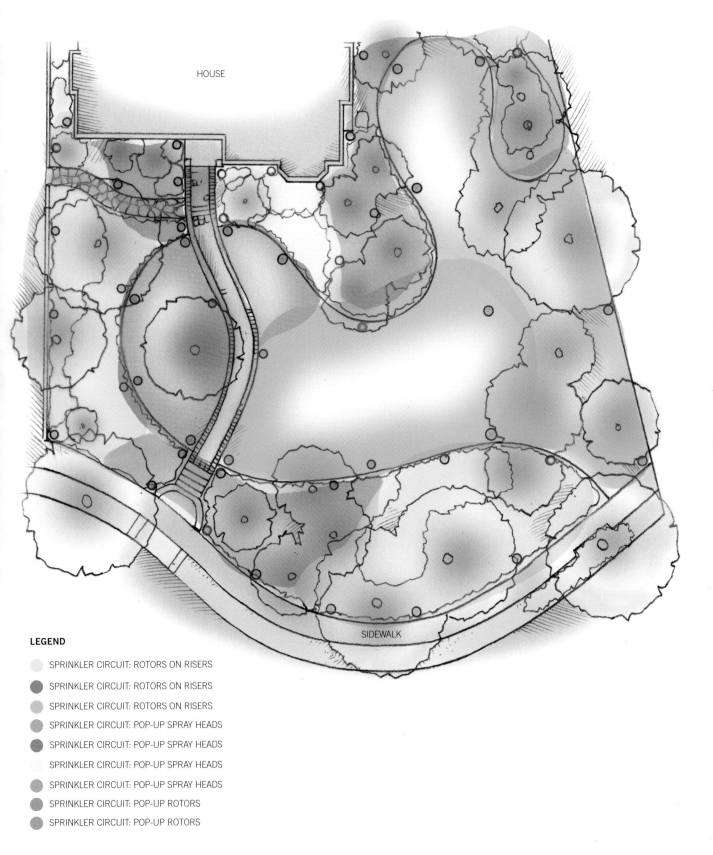

HOUSE

SIDEWALK

LEGEND

- SPRINKLER CIRCUIT: ROTORS ON RISERS
- SPRINKLER CIRCUIT: ROTORS ON RISERS
- SPRINKLER CIRCUIT: ROTORS ON RISERS
- SPRINKLER CIRCUIT: POP-UP SPRAY HEADS
- SPRINKLER CIRCUIT: POP-UP SPRAY HEADS
- SPRINKLER CIRCUIT: POP-UP SPRAY HEADS
- SPRINKLER CIRCUIT: POP-UP SPRAY HEADS
- SPRINKLER CIRCUIT: POP-UP ROTORS
- SPRINKLER CIRCUIT: POP-UP ROTORS

a hillside of natives

This drought-tolerant hillside garden in northern California does not need much water, but it does require regular irrigation during the hot summer months. The small lawn and the planting beds around the house need more frequent watering than the plants on the hill.

The irrigation plan calls for eight circuits: two for drip irrigation and six for the underground sprinkler system. Because of the number of circuits and the distance between hydrozones, the consultant suggests installing a reduced pressure (RP) principle backflow preventer at the main water supply at the front of the house. A single run of PVC pipe can then deliver water to in-line valves at the start of each circuit.

Given the size of the hillside, this plan calls for several circuits of rotors along the top and middle of the slope. The rotors can be placed on 12-inch pop-up bodies or on stationary risers.

(For a house with a slower flow rate, another circuit might be necessary.)

The small lawn area (light purple and yellow) on the right side of the house, however, can be watered with 6-inch pop-up spray heads with a 12- to 15-foot range. Two circuits are needed for the spray heads. Drip lines water all the flower beds (dark green and light green), using a combination of individual emitters and runs of ¼-inch emitter line.

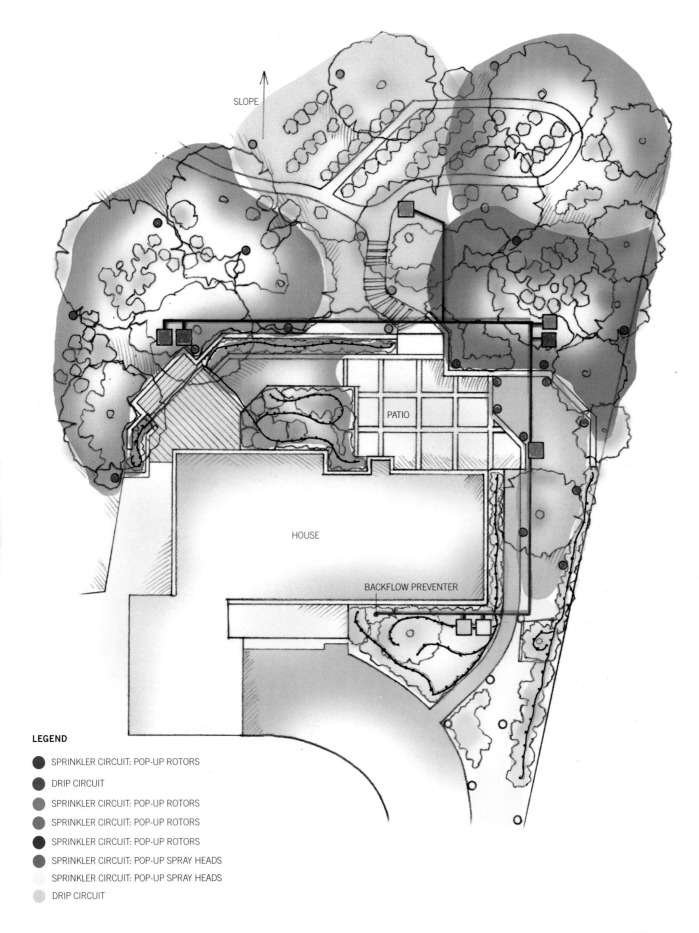

SLOPE

PATIO

HOUSE

BACKFLOW PREVENTER

LEGEND

- SPRINKLER CIRCUIT: POP-UP ROTORS
- DRIP CIRCUIT
- SPRINKLER CIRCUIT: POP-UP ROTORS
- SPRINKLER CIRCUIT: POP-UP ROTORS
- SPRINKLER CIRCUIT: POP-UP ROTORS
- SPRINKLER CIRCUIT: POP-UP SPRAY HEADS
- SPRINKLER CIRCUIT: POP-UP SPRAY HEADS
- DRIP CIRCUIT

a shaded rock garden

Ornamental grasses, baby's tears, and other low-growing plants sit under the canopies of Japanese maples in this well-planned front garden. Given its small size and variety of low, medium, and tall plants and trees, a drip system is the ideal way to irrigate the entire yard.

Although there are many plants throughout this garden, the area can be served by a single drip circuit. The ½-inch drip tubing runs from a battery-operated timer and head assembly at the front of the house into the garden beds. Lengths of ½-inch emitter line with 12-inch emitter spacing lead off the main drip line to snake through plants in the middle of the garden. Shorter lengths of ¼-inch emitter line deliver water to individual plants farther away. Additional watering devices are plugged into the main line to water larger trees and shrubs as needed.

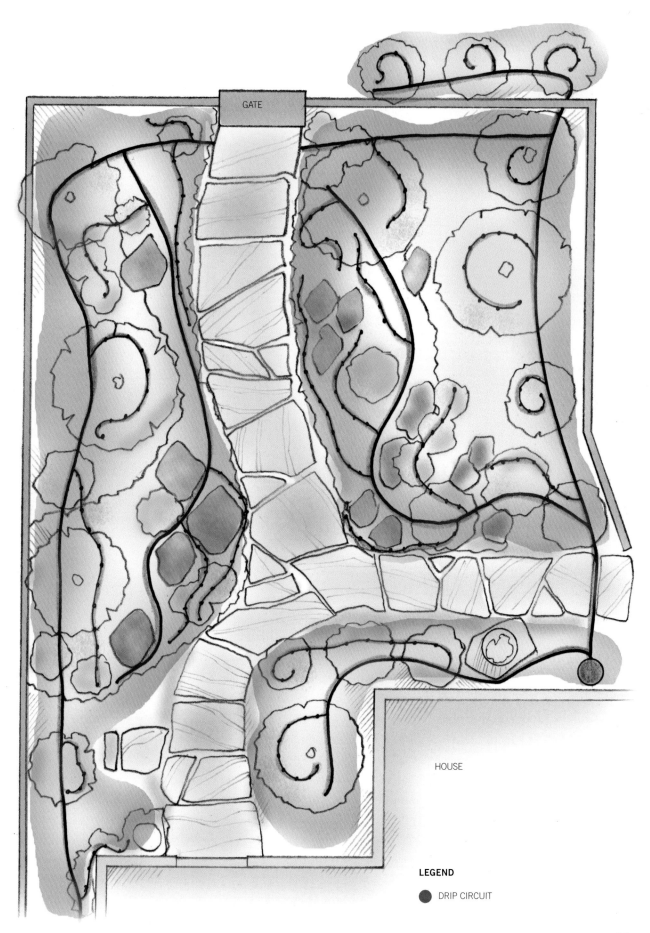

GATE

HOUSE

LEGEND

● DRIP CIRCUIT

a lush country retreat

Set below a high peak in a Rocky Mountain area that gets erratic summer rain, this lush and rambling garden can be watered with just two drip circuits—one for in-ground plants (blue) and one for the potted variety (purple).

Solid ½-inch drip tubing supplies water to the entire landscape. One main drip line runs between the individual pots that line the path and hang from the arbor. Microtubing runs from the main line into each pot, where one or two individual emitters are inserted at the ends of the microtubing, depending on the size of the pot. The other main line snakes around the entire landscape. Individual emitters are inserted into the tubing as necessary and lengths of ¼-inch emitter line run throughout the garden beds and between most of the flagstones in the path.

Given the inconsistent climate in this locale, our consultant also suggests a timer with a rain sensor so the system will turn off automatically when Mother Nature has supplied adequate irrigation.

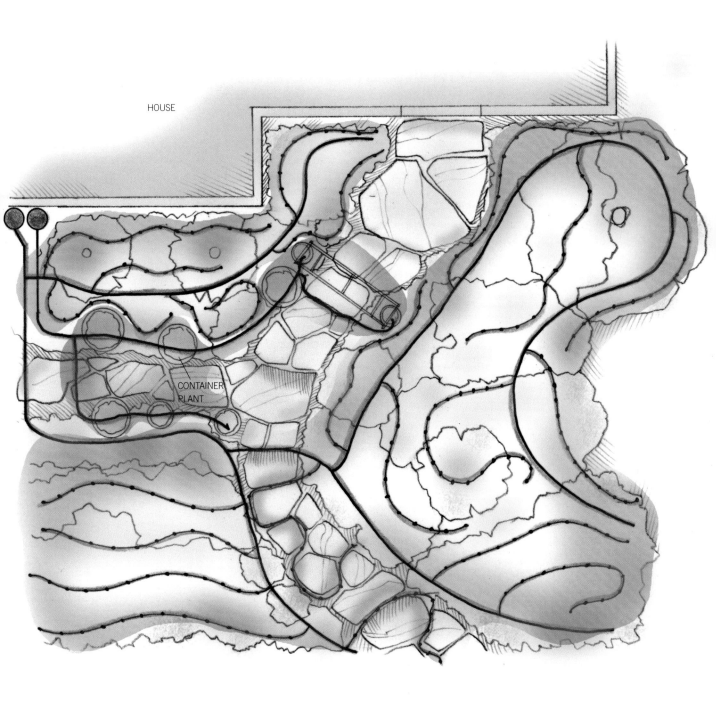

HOUSE

CONTAINER
PLANT

LEGEND

● DRIP CIRCUIT FOR IN-GROUND PLANTS

● DRIP CIRCUIT FOR CONTAINER PLANTS

Credits

PHOTOGRAPHY

William D. Adams: 75; **Em Ahart:** 12 top right, 21 bottom right, 27 bottom, 37 left, 38 left (all), 45 right, 50 bottom, 64, 69 bottom right, 71 top, 72 bottom, 73 top right, 81 middle, 81 bottom; **Marion Brenner:** 83 bottom right, 90; **Karen Bussolini/Positive Images:** 7 right, 23 right; **Crandall & Crandall:** 2, 8, 35 bottom right, 38 right, 43 bottom, 50 top right, 53 bottom left, 59; **Alan & Linda Detrick:** 7 left; **Dig Corporation:** 5 bottom right, 16 top, 17 top, 63 bottom; **Laura Dunkin-Hubby:** 3 top, 3 middle, 10, 11 top, 11 bottom, 12 top left, 12 bottom middle, 12 bottom right, 13, 15 middle, 15 bottom, 16 bottom left, 17 bottom, 18, 19 top, 46, 57 right (all), 62 top, 66 bottom, 67 bottom, 78 bottom right, 79, 80 bottom; **Roger Foley:** 86; **Frank Gaglione:** 83 bottom left, 84; **Saxon Holt:** 5 top, 9, 25 top, 53 top, 60 bottom, 69 bottom left, 71 bottom, 83 top, 88, 96; **Jerry Howard/Positive Images:** 22, 27 top; **Hunter Industries:** 4, 5 bottom left, 12 top left, 19 bottom, 47, 68, 76 bottom; **Ben Klaffke:** 36; **Chas. McGrath:** 21 top, 24 top; **Norman A. Plate:** 16 bottom right, 52, 62 bottom right, 66 top, 70; **Norm Plate:** 82, 92; **Raindrip:** 15 top; **Ian Reeves:** 58 left; **Susan A. Roth:** 24 bottom, 60 top; **Mark Rutherford:** 14, 30, 43 top, 58 right: **Loren Santow:** 62 bottom left, 63 top, 81 top; **Richard Shiell:** 28, 80 top; **Mark R. Statham:** 3 bottom, 11 middle, 34, 35 top, 43 top, 43 middle, 44, 45 left, 48 top, 51, 57 left, 67 top, 69 top, 72 top, 73 top left, bottom, 76 top, 78 top; **Thomas J. Story:** 21 bottom left, 25 bottom, 53 bottom right, 61, 63 top; **Michael S. Thompson:** 12 bottom left, 20, 23 left, 31, 37 right; **Deidra Walpole Photography:** 1; **Tom Wyatt:** 35 bottom left, 48 bottom, 49, 50 top left.

DESIGN

Maile Arnold: 21 top, 24 top; **Heather Hardcastle, Breaking Ground Landscape Designs:** 83 bottom left, 84; **Huettl-Thuilot Associates:** 83 top, 88; **Tom Mannion:** 86; **Judy Ogden:** 60; **Site Design Associates:** 23 right; **Randall Speck:** 23 left; **Urban Farmer:** 21 bottom left, 25 bottom, 53 bottom right, 61; **Tom Wilhite:** 83 bottom right, 90.

Index

Page numbers in **boldface** refer to photographs and illustrations. *Italicized* references indicate boxed text and tables or charts.